Word 2002

Level 2

Cindy Caldwell

Word 2002: Level 2

Part Number: 084301

ACKNOWLEDGMENTS

Project Team

Curriculum Developer and Technical Writer: Cindy Caldwell • **Development Assistance:** Chris Blocher • **Copy Editor:** Rachel Chaffee • **Technical Reviewer:** : Tacha Watson • **Technical Editor:** Rachel Chaffee • **Quality Assurance Analyst:** • **Print Designer:** Daniel Smith • **Content Manager:** Cheryl Russo

Administration

Director of Content and Content Development: William Ingle • **Director of Certification:** Mike Grakowsky • **Director of Design and Web Development:** Joy Insinna • **Manager of Office Productivity and Applied Learning:** Cheryl Russo • **Manager of Databases, ERP, and Business Skills:** Mark Onisk • **Director of Business Development:** Kent Michels • **Manager of Publishing Services:** Michael Hoyt

NOTICES

HELP US IMPROVE OUR COURSEWARE

Your comments are important to us. Please contact us at Element K Press LLC, 1-800-478-7788, 500 Canal View Boulevard, Rochester, NY 14623, Attention: Product Planning, or through our Web site at **http://support.elementkpress.com**.

WORD 2002: LEVEL 2

CONTENTS

LESSON 6: CREATING A WEB PAGE

LESSON 7: MANAGING DOCUMENT CHANGES

NOTES

ABOUT THIS COURSE

Welcome to Microsoft Word 2002: Level 2. This course is the second in a series of three Microsoft Word 2002 courses. By taking this course, you will expand upon the basic concepts that you learned in the Microsoft Word 2002: Level 1 course as well as be introduced to new intermediate concepts with an opportunity to apply them.

Now that you know the basics for creating, editing, and printing Microsoft Word documents, you are ready to gain some intermediate Word skills for performing your job. In this course you will learn about features that save you time and allow you to work smarter.

Course Description

Target Student

This course is designed for persons interested in learning the intermediate features of Word 2002. It is also intended for those preparing to pursue certification as Microsoft Office User Specialists (MOUS) in Word.

Course Prerequisites

Students enrolling in this course should be familiar with personal computers, and know how to use Word 2002 to create, edit, format, and print standard business documents complete with tables. To ensure your success, we recommend you first take the following Element K course or have equivalent knowledge:

- Windows 2000: Introduction
- Word 2002: Level 1

How To Use This Book

As a Learning Guide

Each lesson covers one broad topic or set of related topics. Lessons are arranged in order of increasing proficiency with *Microsoft Word*; skills you acquire in one lesson are used and developed in subsequent lessons. For this reason, you should work through the lessons in sequence.

We organized each lesson into explanatory topics and step-by-step activities. Topics provide the theory you need to master *Microsoft Word*, activities allow you to apply this theory to practical hands-on examples.

You get to try out each new skill on a specially prepared sample file. This saves you typing time and allows you to concentrate on the technique at hand. Through the use of sample files, hands-on activities, illustrations that give you feedback at crucial steps, and supporting background information, this book provides you with the foundation and structure to learn *Microsoft Word* quickly and easily.

As a Review Tool

Any method of instruction is only as effective as the time and effort you are willing to invest in it. For this reason, we encourage you to spend some time reviewing the book's more challenging topics and activities.

As a Reference

You can use the Concepts sections in this book as a first source for definitions of terms, background information on given topics, and summaries of procedures.

Course Objectives

In this course, you will use Microsoft Word intermediate features for creating custom templates and styles, managing tables and table data, inserting graphics, creating a newsletter, sending form letters, creating a Web page, and managing document changes.

You will:

- create and modify custom templates, apply existing styles, and create a custom style.

- enhance a table by merging table cells, sorting and calculating table data, and creating charts based on various table data.

- learn how to insert, manipulate, and format graphic images, including clip art, AutoShapes, WordArt, and organization charts.

- create a newsletter using columns, sections, and graphics.

- use the Mail Merge Wizard to mail merge form letters, complete with mailing labels.

- create a Web page, create and edit a hyperlink, save and preview a Web page, as well as enhance a Web page by applying themes.

- include comments in a document and compare and merge documents.

Course Requirements

Hardware:

- Pentium 133 MHz or higher processor required for all operating systems.

- 64 MB of RAM recommended minimum for Windows 2000 Professional; in addition, you should have 8 MB of RAM for each application running simultaneously. (Note: Memory requirements may differ for other operating systems).

- 600 MB of free hard disk space. (Under Windows 2000, at least 4 MB of space must be available in the registry.)
- Either a local CD-ROM drive or access to a networked CD-ROM driver for installation purposes.
- A floppy-disk drive.
- A two-button mouse, an IntelliMouse, or compatible pointing device.
- VGA or higher resolution monitor; Super VGA recommended.
- An installed printer driver. (Printers are not required; however, each PC must have an installed printer driver to use Print Preview.)
- An Internet connection is required in order to complete some tasks for this class; therefore, you will need a 9600 baud modem or higher.
- If you plan to key optional Activity 5–2 "Performing a Mail Merge Using Outlook Contacts" in Lesson 5 of this course, you will require a Microsoft Exchange Server. See the Class Setup section for details.

Software:

- A complete installation of Microsoft Office XP Professional—see the Class Setup Requirements for additional instructions.

Software:

- If you plan to key optional Activity 5–2 "Performing a Mail Merge Using Outlook Contacts" in Lesson 5 of this course, you will require a Microsoft Exchange Server. Microsoft Exchange, Internet SMTP/POP3, IMAP4, or other MAPI-compliant messaging software required for e-mail features.
- Windows 2000 Professional. This book was written using the Windows 2000 Professional operating system. Using this book with other operating systems may affect how the activities work. Note: The manufacturer states that Microsoft Office XP Professional with FrontPage will work with Microsoft Windows 98, Microsoft Windows ME, and Microsoft Windows NT Workstation 4.0. Office XP Professional with FrontPage will not run on the Microsoft Windows 3.x, Microsoft Windows NT 3.5x, or Microsoft Windows 95 operating systems.

Class Setup

1. Install Windows 2000 Professional on a newly formatted hard drive.
2. If the Getting Started with Windows 2000 window is displayed, uncheck "Show this screen at startup." and click Exit.
3. Install a print driver. A printer isn't necessary for class, but you must have a printer driver installed.
4. Perform a complete installation of Microsoft Office XP Professional. If you choose not to install all of the Office applications, some of activities in this book may not work correctly.

5. Verify that file extensions are visible. (In Windows Explorer, choose View→Folder Options and select the View tab. If necessary, uncheck the Hide File Extensions For Known File Types options and click on OK.)

6. Minimize the Language bar.

7. In Word, open the thesaurus to install it.

8. Verify that the Internet connection works.

9. The steps above need to be done only once. The steps below must be done before every class to ensure a proper setup.

10. On the student's computers, reset the usage data. (Choose Tools→Customize and click Reset My Usage Data to restore the default settings.)

11. Run the self-extracting data file located on the data disk. This will place the data in the My Documents folder.

12. If you plan to key optional Activity 5–2 "Performing a Mail Merge Using Outlook Contacts" in Lesson 5 of this course, you will also need to perform the following setup steps:

13. Configure Outlook 2002: Double-click on the Microsoft Outlook shortcut on the Windows desktop.

14. In the Outlook 2002 Startup dialog box, click Next.

15. In the Account Configuration dialog box, E-mail Accounts, select Yes to configure an e-mail account, and click Next.

16. In the E-mail Accounts dialog box, Server Type, select Microsoft Exchange Server, and click Next.

17. In the Exchange Server Settings, Microsoft Exchange Server text box, type the name of the server you are using. In the User Name text box, type the user name. Click Next.

18. Click Finish to close the Wizard.

19. In the Enter Password dialog box, type the user name, password, and domain name, and click OK.

20. If an alert is displayed stating that the Microsoft Exchange Server is unavailable, click Retry.

21. On the Exchange Server, if necessary, delete all user names on the Exchange server.

22. On the Exchange Server, create a user name for the instructor (student00) and for each student in the class (starting with student01). You may wish to provide place cards identifying each computer's user name (student##).

23. Log on to Windows using the student user name.

24. Finally, drag the nine contact data files provided in the Contacts folder on the data disk to the Outlook Contacts folder.

LESSON 1
Creating and Modifying Templates

Data Files:
About Us.doc
Burke Memo.doc

Lesson Time:
30–40 minutes

Lesson Objectives:

In this lesson, you will create and modify custom templates, apply existing styles, and create a custom style.

You will:

* apply styles to document text.
* modify an existing style.
* create and apply a custom style.
* create a custom template based on an existing document.

Introduction

Welcome to Microsoft Word 2002. As you probably know, Word ships with a variety of templates, including global templates and document templates, and that using templates can save you time by acting as a pattern, providing the structure, common content, and settings that help you shape a final document. In this first lesson you will apply some of Word's "built-in" formatting to text as well as create, apply, and delete your own groups of formatting effects. You will also expand your knowledge of templates by creating and modifying a custom template for your personal use.

Although Word comes with a wide variety of templates that allow you to create new documents with a standard look, there may be times when you need a custom template that applies to your organizations specific needs. Perhaps you create countless memos that include the company name, logo, and standard address components. To save time, you can create your own custom templates that includes those elements. You may also want to apply built-in formatting to your custom template, or create your own built-in formats. You can then create a new document based on this custom template, using built-in formats, at any time.

TOPIC A

Apply Styles

You have probably applied various character and paragraph formatting within your documents. For example, you may have applied a bold format to a word or changed a paragraph alignment. In any event, you know that the overall effectiveness of a document is directly related to the way it looks. Word offers an alternative for applying formatting—sets of formatting instructions that can be applied quickly to affect text. In this topic you will apply "built-in" Word formatting options in order to apply groups of character and paragraph formatting to text all at once.

Suppose you apply an Arial, 16 point font, and then apply bold to the majority of headings in your business documents. While the Format Painter is a helpful tool for copying formats, it's faster to bundle all of these formatting effects together and apply them all at one time. Word's style feature allows you to do just that!

Styles

Microsoft Word allows you to group formats together and then apply them all at once using the styles feature.

Definition: A *style* is a set of formatting characteristics that can be applied quickly to format text, tables, and lists in your document automatically and consistently. Table 1-1 lists the types of styles you can create and apply, what each type controls within a document, and how they are identified graphically within Word style lists. Word provides several basic "built-in" styles to get you started, however, you can also create your own "user-defined styles" to include basic and special formatting such as paragraph spacing and borders.

Table 1-1: *Types of Styles.*

Style Type	Controls	Identifier

Paragraph Style	Controls a paragraph's appearance, such as text alignment, tab stops, spacing, and borders. Paragraph styles can include character styles.	¶
Character Style	Controls the appearance of selected text within a paragraph, such as font and size of text, and bold and italic formats.	<u>a</u>
Table Style	Provides a consistent look to borders, shading, alignment, and fonts in tables.	⊞
List Style	Applies similar alignment, numbering or bullet characters, and fonts to lists.	☰

Example: Some built in style examples include: Normal, Heading 1, Heading 2, Page Number, and Table 3D Effects 1.

Analogy: Think of a style as a recipe for formatting text. Rather than using eggs and flour to make a cake, you'll be using a variety of formats to make a style.

The Normal Style Word generally starts a document with the *Normal* paragraph style applied. By default, the Normal style sets the font (Times New Roman), style (regular), size (12 point), color (automatic [black]), and paragraph alignment (left) for every new document.

The Styles and Formatting Task Pane

Word offers several tools for applying styles. You can apply styles using the Formatting toolbar's Style box, as shown in Figure 1-1; or you can use the Styles and Formatting task pane. In this topic you will use the Styles and Formatting task pane, shown in Figure 1-2, since it offers more options.

Times New Roman ▾

Figure 1-1: *The Style box.*

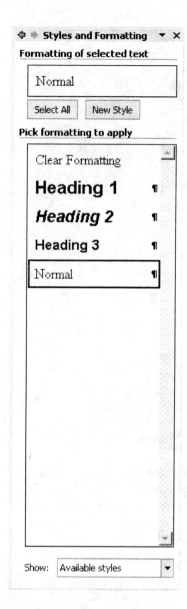

Figure 1-2: *The Styles and Formatting task pane.*

The advantage of using the Styles and Formatting task pane is that Word will keep track of all of your formats so you can quickly reapply them. The Styles and Formatting task pane also allows you to create, view, and modify styles. To display the Styles and Formatting task pane, choose one of the following techniques:

*   On the Formatting toolbar, click on the Styles and Formatting button .

*   Choose Format, Styles and Formatting.

*   From the Styles drop-down list, select More.

*   From the Task Pane title bar drop-down list, select Styles and Formatting.

The Reveal Formatting task pane

Word offers several tools for viewing applied styles. The Reveal Formatting task pane is one tool that displays the current font, paragraph, spacing, image, table properties, and more, at any point in your document. It enables you to do the following:

*   Change formatting properties—click the text with a blue underline to display the associated dialog box and make any desired changes.

- Distinguish a style source—check this check box to determine whether the formatting came from a style.

- Show formatting marks—check the Show All Formatting Marks check box to show paragraph marks and tabs.

- Apply formatting to surrounding text—in the Selected text box, click the arrow, and then click the Apply Formatting Of Surrounding Text to format a text selection like the text that surrounds it.

The Style Area

Another tool for displaying applied styles is the Style Area, shown in Figure 1-3. You can have Word display the name of each paragraph's style in a separate style area at the left of the document window—in Normal or Outline view only. The Style Area can help you determine whether or not text has been manually formatted, or perhaps whether there have been default or custom styles applied to it.

Normal	
Normal	We'll Find The Right Property For You
Heading 2	**About Us**
Normal	*Burke Properties* was founded as, and continues to be, a full-service real estate brokerage firm. We provide a broad range of real estate services including residential and commercial sales and leasing. Jan Burke, the President, has been personally involved in all phases of real estate for over twenty years. This experience includes: historic preservation, restoration, leasing and sales management, and consulting for developers on issues ranging from planning to final marketing. Our brokers and associates are a well-balanced team of seasoned professionals who offer our clients a unique blend of specialties in the various markets within the area.
Normal	
Heading 2	**Description of our Firm**
Normal	*Burke Properties* offers a functional delivery service around a true single point of contact, with a team of experienced, diverse professionals. Our point of difference from other firms may be that our caseloads are limited; when you need help, the person you need to talk to is the person you "get" to. We are customer driven, while being a competitive, proactive leader in providing services. We have positioned ourselves in the community as being both flexible toward and adaptive to the varying cultures and needs of our clients.
Normal	
Heading 2	**Our Goal**
Normal	The goal of *Burke Properties* is to provide the best customized, diverse service to our clients. We realize that quality service is the key to our business. We strive to earn your respect through an honest, fair, and direct approach to your real estate needs. By realizing our goal, we will meet your needs now and in the future. We will be rewarded with your recommendations to your family, friends, and business associates.

Figure 1-3: *A document window with the Style Area displayed.*

To display the Style Area:

1. In an open document, switch to Normal view, if necessary.

2. Choose Tools→Options.

3. On the View tab, increase the Style Area Width to an appropriate measurement—one that will accommodate longer style names in your document, 1 for example.

ACTIVITY 1-1

Orientation to the Styles and Formatting Task Pane

Activity Time:
5 minutes

Objective:	To become acquainted with the Styles and Formatting task pane.
Setup:	Word is running with no files open, and nonprinting symbols are displayed. (On the Standard toolbar, click on the Show/Hide button ¶).
Setup:	All course data files are located in the C:\My Documents folder.
Scenario:	You work as an administrative assistant to Jan Burke, the President of Burke Properties, a successful real estate company. Your company uses Microsoft Word 2002 software for all of your word processing needs. You manager has asked that you apply some of Words built-in styles to the document About Us.doc. Because you haven't worked with styles before, you open the document and display the Styles and Formatting task pane in order to get acquainted with it.

What You Do	How You Do It
1. With About Us.doc open **display the Styles and Formatting task pane.**	a. **Open** About Us.doc.
	b. On the Formatting toolbar, **click on the Styles and Formatting button** 𝒜 .
	🖋 You can also display the Task pane drop-down list and select Styles and Formatting to display the Styles and Formatting task pane.
	c. **Position your insertion point within the "About Us" heading.**
2. **What Style is applied to the heading "About Us?"**	

3. **Display the details of the formats associated with the Heading 1 style and the available menu choices.**

a. **Point to the Formatting Of Selected Text text box** to display the screen tip for the Heading 1 style.

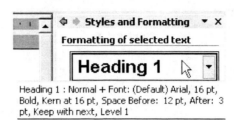

b. With the screen tip visible, **click the drop-down arrow** to display the menu.

4. **What are some of the available options from the Formatting of Selected Text drop-down menu?**

To view detailed formatting information for a style, choose Reveal Formatting from the Formatting Of Selected Text list box's drop-down menu. This will display the Reveal Formatting task pane.

5. **Use the Show list drop-down menu to display various groups of formatting styles in the Pick Formatting To Apply list.**

When you're finished, **return the Show list to the default of Available Formatting.**

a. **Observe the styles listed in the Pick Formatting To Apply list.** The list shows available formatting.

b. Near the bottom of the task pane, **observe the Show list box.** This box specifies which types of styles and formatting to show under Pick Formatting To Apply.

c. **Display the Show list drop-down list and while observing the Pick Formatting To Apply list, select each of the following menu choices:**

Formatting in Use

Available Styles

All Styles

d. **Return the Show list to display Available Formatting.**

Apply Styles

Procedure Reference

To apply a style:

1. Select the text you want to format with a character style; or place the insertion point in the paragraph, table, or list that you want to format with a style.

    ✏ To apply a paragraph style to several paragraphs, select at least a portion of all the paragraphs to be formatted.

2. Choose a style from the Style box or from the Styles and Formatting task pane.

ACTIVITY 1-2

Applying Styles

Setup: About Us.doc is open. The Styles and Formatting task pane is displayed.

Scenario: Now that you're familiar with the Styles and Formatting task pane, you go ahead and apply styles as your manager requested. You apply two different built in Word styles to text in the document in order to enhance it. After applying the styles, you save the file as My About Us.doc.

What You Do	How You Do It
1. Apply the Heading 2 paragraph style to the three heading paragraphs.	a. Using your mouse, **point in the white space to the left of the heading "About Us."** When your mouse pointer appears as a **right-pointing arrow, click** to select the heading.
	b. **Press [Ctrl] and click in the white space to the left of the heading "Description of our Firm"** to select both headings at once.
	c. **Press [Ctrl] and click in the white space to the left of the heading "Our Goal"** to select all three headings.
	d. In the Styles and Formatting task pane, under Pick Formatting To Apply, **select Heading 2.**

2. In the Pick Formatting To Apply list, display all available styles and apply the Emphasis character style to all occurrences of the text "Burke Properties."

   a. From the Show list drop-down menu, **choose All Styles.**

   b. In the document, **select the three occurrences of Burke Properties.** (All three reside in the first sentence of each paragraph.)

   c. In the task pane, under Pick Formatting To Apply, **scroll to select Emphasis.**

3. **Display and observe the Style Area in Normal view.**

   a. **Choose Tools→Options,** and if necessary, **select the View tab.**

   b. Near the bottom of the view tab, under Outline and Normal options, **enter .8 into the Style Area Width box.**

   c. **Click OK.**

   d. **Choose View→Normal.**

   🖉 You can quickly size or remove the style area by dragging the border appropriately.

   e. **Choose View→Print Layout.**

   f. **Save the file as** My About Us.doc.

TOPIC B

Modify Styles

Now that you know what a style is and how to apply them, know that they are just like everything else in the world—subject to change. Word gives you the ability to modify any of the styles to which your document has access. In this topic you will learn how to modify styles.

Suppose you want to change the Heading 3 style to be italicized. Rather than italicize each instance of the Heading 3 style by hand, you can simply modify the style to include italic formatting, thereby changing all instances of Heading 3 simultaneously.

Modify Styles

Modifying a Style Using Example Text.

You can modify styles in one of two ways: using example text or using the Modify Style dialog box. Using example text is faster, however, it doesn't offer as many options as using the Modify Style dialog box. To modify a paragraph or character style using example text:

1. Select the example text that has the style you want to modify.

   🖈 To save time, select text with formatting that is as close as possible to the formatting you want to assign to the style.

2. Modify the selected text's formatting as desired.

3. Display the Styles and Formatting task pane.

4. Locate the name of the style you're modifying in the Pick Formatting To Apply list.

5. Click on the down arrow that appears when you move the mouse pointer over the style name, and choose Update To Match Selection form the drop-down menu.

Modifying a Style Using the Modify Style Dialog Box

To modify a style using the Modify Style dialog box:

1. Display the Styles and Formatting task pane.

2. In the Pick Formatting To Apply list, locate the name of the style you're modifying.

3. Click on the down arrow that appears when you move the mouse pointer over the style name, and choose Modify form the drop-down menu.

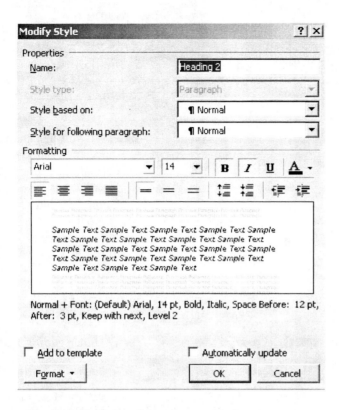

Figure 1-4: *The Modify Styles dialog box.*

4. Using the various dialog box options, as show in Figure 1-4, make your modifications.

5. Click OK to save your modifications.

ACTIVITY 1-3

Modifying a Style

Setup: My About Us.doc is open in Print Layout view. The Styles and Formatting task pane is open.

Scenario: Now that you have applied the Heading 2 style to the paragraph headings in the My About Us.doc, your manager decides that the headings would look better if they were underlined. So, you modify the Heading 2 style to include underlining. When finished, you save the file.

What You Do	How You Do It
1. Display the Modify Style dialog box for the Heading 2 style.	a. In the Pick Formatting To Apply list, **click on the down arrow that appears when you move the mouse pointer over the style name Heading 2.**
	● When you display the style's drop-down menu in the Styles and Formatting task pane, be sure to click the down arrow and not the style name. Clicking on the style name will immediately remove any applied formatting and apply the unmodified style to the text.
	b. **Choose Modify.**
2. Modify the Heading 2 style to include underlining.	a. **Verify that Heading 2 appears in the Name box.**
	b. In the Modify Style dialog box, under Formatting, **click on the Underline button** **U** .
	c. **Click on OK.**
	d. **Observe the paragraph headings.** They are now underlined. When applied, the Heading 2 style will now apply underlining.
3. What has changed in the document?	
Save the file.	

TOPIC C

Create User-Defined Styles

It is unlikely that the few common styles that Word provides will meet all of your style needs, therefore, you may wish to create your own custom styles for functionality and variety. In this topic you will learn to create user-defined paragraph and character styles.

If you find yourself applying the same set of formatting features to characters or paragraphs, it's time to create a new user-defined style. For example, you may frequently emphasize words by applying a 16–point font and a blue font color, you could define a character style—named Large Blue.

Create User-Defined Styles

Creating a Style Using the New Style Dialog Box

Just like modifying an existing style, you can create a new style in one of two ways—using example text or using the New Style dialog box. To create a new style using the New Style dialog box:

1. Display the Styles and Formatting task pane.

2. Under Formatting Of Selected Text, click on New Style to display the New Style dialog box.

3. Name the style and select a style type (paragraph, character, table, or list.)

4. Click Format and adjust the desired settings (font, paragraph, tabs, borders, and so on.)

5. Click OK twice to format the style and to create the new style.

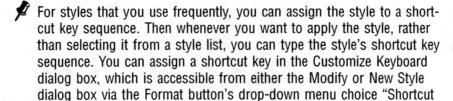 For styles that you use frequently, you can assign the style to a short-cut key sequence. Then whenever you want to apply the style, rather than selecting it from a style list, you can type the style's shortcut key sequence. You can assign a shortcut key in the Customize Keyboard dialog box, which is accessible from either the Modify or New Style dialog box via the Format button's drop-down menu choice "Shortcut Key."

Creating a Style by Example

To create a new style by example:

1. Select example text that is as close as possible to the style that you want to create.

2. Apply any desired formatting.

3. Follow steps 1–5 given in the procedure for creating a user-defined style with the New Styles dialog box.

Deleting a Style

When deleting files, there are a few things to keep in mind. Even though you can modify styles provided by Word—Normal and Heading 1, for example—you can't delete them. You can only delete user-defined styles. Additionally, when you delete a custom style, any text that had that deleted style applied to it reverts to the Normal style.

To delete a user-defined style:

1. In the Styles and Formatting task pane, locate the style you want to delete.

2. Click on the down arrow that appears when you move the mouse pointer over the style name that you wish to delete, and choose Delete from the drop-down menu.

3. Click Yes when Word asks whether you want to delete the style.

📌 To delete multiple styles quickly and efficiently, you can use the Organizer. Simply select the style to delete, and press Delete.

ACTIVITY 1-4

Creating User-Defined Styles

Setup: My About Us.doc is open. The Styles and Formatting task pane is displayed.

Scenario: You decide that My About Us.doc could use a centered heading of Burke Properties. Because you want all Burke Properties heading occurrences to have the same look throughout all of your documents, you decide to create a new style called BP Head using the New Style dialog box, where you set various formatting, spacing, and text flow attributes. Once you have created such an effective style for your company name, you create a user-defined character style for use in formatting Jan Burke's name and title. Finally you save and close the file.

1. Use the I-beam to center the line above "We'll Find The Right Property For You."	a. Click before the return symbol at the top of the document.
	b. Position the I-beam on the center of the line above "We'll Find The Right Property For" until a center symbol appears below the I-beam..

We'll·Find·The·Right·Property·For·You¶

	c. **Double-click** to set the insertion point in the center of the line. (Use the horizontal ruler as a guide to position the mouse pointer 3" in from the left.)

2. In the New Style dialog box create a new style called *BP Head* that has the paragraph style attributes shown in Figure 1-5	a. Under Formatting of Selected Text, **click New Style** New Style .
	b. In the Name field, type *BP Head*.
	📌 It is a good idea to precede your custom style names with characters that set them apart from Word's default styles. In this example, BP stands for Burke Properties.
	c. Under Formatting, **select Arial, 28 point, Bold.**

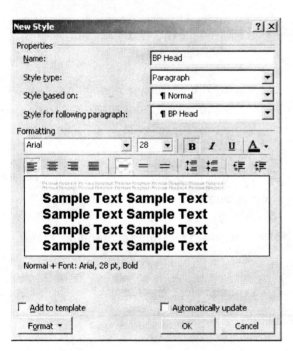

Figure 1-5: *The New Style dialog box.*

3. **Set the following new paragraph attributes:**

   Spacing After: **6 points.**

   Pagination: If necessary, **select Widows and Orphans and select Keep Lines Together.**

   a. In the New Style dialog box, **click on the Format drop-down arrow.**

   b. **Choose Paragraph.**

   c. On the Indents And Spacing tab, **set Spacing After to 6 points.**

   📌 Note that the General Alignment is set to Centered because you used click and type.

   d. On the Line and Page Breaks tab, **select Widow/Orphan Control, if necessary, and select Keep Lines Together.**

   e. **Click OK twice.**

4. **Apply the newly created paragraph style to the paragraph with the insertion point, and type *Burke Properties.***

   a. From the Pick Formatting of Selected Text list, **select BP Head.**

   b. **Type *Burke Properties.***

5. **Create and apply a new character style called BP President with Times New Roman, 12 point, and Italic as the font attributes.** Your style should look something like this:

   Burke·Properties

   a. In the second sentence of the first paragraph, **select the text "Jan Burke, the President."**

   b. **Display the New Style dialog box.**

   c. **Name the character style *BP President.***

   d. If necessary, **select Times New Roman, 12 point, and select Italic as the font attributes.**

   e. **Apply the new style to "Jan Burke, the President."**

   f. **Save and close the file.**

TOPIC D

Create a Template from an Existing Document

As you know, Word templates are great time-savers. In the event that the templates provided in Word don't meet your needs, you can create a custom template to use repeatedly in your day-to-day work.

You may find yourself repeating the same document layout and formatting tasks. Rather than continuing to recreate the wheel, why not create a template that contains the layout and formatting that you use repeatedly so that it will be available to you each time you choose to create a new document?

The Organizer

Procedure Reference

After you've gone to a lot of trouble creating user-defined styles, it would be a shame to waste all that hard work. Thanks to the Organizer tool, you don't have to. Word's *Organizer* tool gives you the ability to manage and share your AutoText entries, styles, toolbars, and macro projects between documents. (For our purposes here, we'll focus on how you can use the Organizer to work with styles.) In short, the Organizer lets you copy, delete, and rename any of these items.

Copying a style between documents or templates is a great way to save time. You simply have to copy the desired project from one document or template to another and then apply the copied style as usual. To copy a style between documents or templates:

1. Choose Tools→Templates and Add-Ins.

2. In the Templates and Add-Ins dialog box, click Organizer

3. If necessary, select the Styles tab.

4. Ensure that the "from" and "to" files—documents or templates—are referenced in the Styles Available In boxes. Use the Close and Open buttons to set these up.

5. Select the styles that you wish to copy.

6. Click Copy and then click Close.

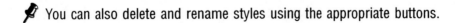 You can also delete and rename styles using the appropriate buttons.

Create a Template from an Existing Document

Procedure Reference

Although you can create a template from scratch, it is more likely that you will create a template based on an existing file. So, when you frequently re-use a document, it is a good idea to create a template of that document so that you don't have to recreate it each time you wish to use it. To do this:

1. Open the document that you wish to base the template on.

2. Remove or replace any custom text and make any formatting changes.

3. Choose File→Save As.

4. In the Save As Type box, select Document Template(*.dot).

5. Name the file.

6. Click Save.

🖈 When you select Document Template (*.dot) from the Save As Type drop-down list box in step 4, Word automatically changes the Save In location to the default Templates folder. Templates you save in the Templates folder appear on the General tab of the Templates dialog box that is displayed by choosing File→New from the menu, and then General Templates from the New Document task pane. We recommend that you avoid changing the default template location, and that your systems administrator store those templates that you share on a network in the Workgroup templates file location.

ACTIVITY 1-5

Creating a Template from an Existing Document

Setup: Word is open with the Styles and Formatting task pane is displayed.

Scenario: Today your manager received a memo, called Burke Memo.doc, that you are very impressed with. It contains formatting, a company logo, a footer, and a layout that you would like to emulate for the memos you generate from the President's office. While creating a new template from the Burke Memo.doc file, you copy user-defined styles stored in another document to the new template file, saving it as My Burke Memo.dot. After testing the template, you close the temporarily named file without saving changes.

Burke·Properties¶

Memo → → → → → ¶

   To: → ¶

   From: → *Jan Burke, President*¶

   CC: → ¶

   Date: → August·22,·2001¶

   Re: → ¶

Figure 1-6: *The completed My Template.dot file.*

What You Do	How You Do It
1. In Burke Memo.doc, what would you change before saving the file as a template file?	
2. **Make the necessary edits to the memo so that your screen matches Figure 1-6.**	a. In Burke Memo.doc, **delete the To, CC:, and Re: text entries, but do not delete the tab or return symbols.** (Leave the Date field as is, since it is set up to automatically update for you.)
	b. Replace Ronald Thomas with *Jan Burke, President*.
	c. Remove all the text below the horizontal line.

3. **In the Styles tab of the Organizer dialog box, perform the steps necessary to have your screen match Figure 1-7 below.**

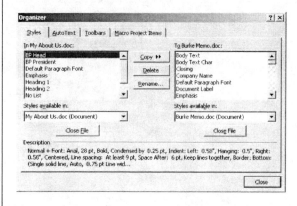

Figure 1-7: *The Organizer dialog box.*

a. **Choose Tools→Templates and Add-Ins.**

b. **Click Organizer** Organizer... **, and if necessary, select the Styles tab.**

c. **On the left side of the Organizer window, click Close File.**

d. **On the left side of the Organizer window, click Open File.**

e. Navigate to the My Documents folder and **open** My About Us.doc. (Be sure to change the Files of Type list to Word Documents(*.doc).

f. **On the right side of the Organizer window, click Close File.**

g. **On the right side of the Organizer window, click Open File.**

h. Navigate to the My Documents folder and **open** Burke Memo.doc. (Be sure to change the Files of Type list to Word Documents(*.doc).

4. **Copy the BP Head and the BP President styles to** Burke Memo.doc.

   Apply the BP President style to the From field text "Jan Burke, President" and the BP Heading style to the heading "Burke Properties."

a. From the In My About Us.doc list, **select both the BP Head and BP President.** (Use the [Ctrl] key.)

b. **Click Copy** Copy ▶▶ **.**

c. **Click Close.** The two user-defined styles are available in the Styles list.

d. **Select the heading text "Burke Properties" and apply the BP Head style.**

e. **Select the text "Jan Burke, President" and apply the BP President style.**

5. You're now ready to save this file as a template file. **Save the file as a template file named** My Burke Memo.dot

   a. In the Save As dialog box, in the File Name text box, **type** *My Burke Memo*.

   b. In the Save As Type drop-down list, **select Document Template(*.dot).**

   c. **Observe the Save In: text box.** Word automatically switches to the default user template location.

   d. **Click Save and observe the active window's title bar.** The existing document was successfully converted into a template My Burke Memo.dot.

---

6. To test your new template, **close the template and display the New Document task pane.**

   Display the Templates dialog box and open the new template file.

   a. **Close the template.**

   b. **Choose File→New.**

   c. In the New Document task pane, under New From Template, **select General Templates.**

   d. In the Templates dialog box, **double-click on** My Burke Memo.dot.

---

7. What type of file appears in the active document window?

---

8. **Suppose that you now want to enter the information for a new memo. Once entered, how would you save this file?**

Close the file.

Lesson 1 Follow-up

If Word's built-in templates don't provide you with exactly what you need, you can create your own custom templates, complete with user-defined styles.

1. **When would you want to create a custom style?**

2. **When might you want to create a custom template?**

Lesson 1: Creating and Modifying Templates

Where are Templates?
Tools
Option
File Location

NOTES

LESSON 2
Managing Tables and Table Data in Documents

Data Files:
Driving Directions.doc
Mortgage Letter.doc
Sort Rates.xls
Loan.doc
Company Results.xls
Marketing Piece.doc

Lesson Time:
50–60 minutes

Lesson Objectives:

In this lesson, you will enhance a table by merging table cells, sorting and calculating table data, and creating charts based on various table data.

You will:

*   convert existing tabbed text into a table.
*   merge the cells of a table to make room for a table title.
*   open an Excel table in Word.
*   sort Word table data.
*   use the Sum formula to perform calculations in a table.
*   create a chart based on Word table data.
*   create a link between an Excel worksheet and a Word table.

Introduction

Tables are an effective tool for making your document information more readable and visually appealing. You know how to insert and revise tables by adding, deleting, and resizing rows and columns. You also know how to format tables by adding borders, shading, or using the AutoFormat feature. In this lesson you will go beyond the basics of creating simple tables and learn to use Word's intermediate table features including converting existing text into a table, rearranging table information, and calculating, charting, and linking table data.

You keep data in tables so that it is easy to digest, update, and keep track of. You already know how to create simple tables, but suppose, for example, you are responsible for managing tables of employees, telephone number lists, or a parts inventory list. These types of data change often, and may even need to be rearranged, calculated, or converted into a chart. Knowing how to manage tables is key to your success in working with them. This lesson will show you all of that and more!

TOPIC A

Convert Tabbed Text into a Table

At times you will create tables for document information, and at other times you may use the tab key to separate document information. After using the tab approach, you may find that a table would work better. In this topic will open an existing document and convert the text into a table so that the data is easier to read and use.

Suppose that you have inherited an employee telephone list that is difficult to work with; one that you are now responsible for keeping up to date. To make it easier to read and use, you decide to convert the data to a table. It's easy to do in Word!

Convert Existing Tabbed Text into a Table

Procedure Reference

A common way to arrange text into a table-like format, simulating columns, is to use tabbed text. Simply put, when you separate text with tabs, you've created tabbed text. (Arranging data in columns using tabs is a hold over from the days of typewriters.) A much more flexible way to organize text and graphics into columns is to convert tabbed text into a table. It's best to convert tabbed text into tables when you have existing information that needs to be frequently updated. To convert tabbed text into a table:

1. Select all tabbed text that you want to be included in the table.

2. Choose Table→Convert→Text To Table.

3. In the Convert Text To Table dialog box, shown in Figure 2-1, select the desired settings.

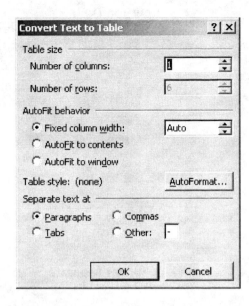

Figure 2-1: *The Convert Text to Table dialog box.*

4.   Click OK.

> 📌 You can convert a table back into tabbed text by selecting the table and choosing Table→Convert→Table To Text.

ACTIVITY 2-1

Converting Tabbed Text into a Table

Setup: Word is open with no files open.

Scenario: Because you are the administrative assistant to the President of Burke Proper-ties, you receive many requests for driving directions to your home office. Rather than verbally repeating these directions, you decide to create a file for distribution. Though you are aware of a driving directions file created by your predecessor, you recall that it was a bit hard to read. Rather than starting from scratch, you decide to investigate the electronic file named Driving Directions.doc. Once opened, you notice that your predecessor didn't create this data in a table. To make the directions easier to read you decide to convert the tabbed text into a table to make the directions easier to follow. When finished, save the file as My Driving Directions.doc.

LESSON 2

What You Do	How You Do It
1. In Driving Directions.doc convert all of the text to a 3 column table, with a fixed column width, separating text at tabs.	a. **Open** Driving Directions.doc.
	b. **Select all of the document text.** (Press [Ctrl]+A).
	c. **Choose Table→Convert→Text to Table.**
	d. **Set the Number of Columns to 3.**
	e. **Verify that the Fixed Column Width is set to Auto.**
	f. **Under Separate Text At, select Tabs.**
	g. **Click on OK.**

2. **How does this table compare with the tabbed driving directions?**

Save the file as My Driving Directions.doc

TOPIC B

Merge Cells in a Table

It's important that you identify your table data so that users will know what the data within your table represents. By adding a header row, you can label your table so that it makes more sense to your audience. In this topic you will learn the steps necessary to create and position a header row in a table, and how to merge cells within a row.

Because you want to identify the information in your tables, it's important to add heading information to them. When you convert tabbed text to a table, you might end up with a row of data with text in only the first cell. If this data is a heading, it can look out of place. In this situation, you would merge the cells so that the row would consist of just one cell. This is called merging cells and it is easy to do in a Word table.

Merge Cells in a Table

Procedure Reference

Being able to merge table cells is helpful for accommodating long strings of numbers or words, such as a table title or a column heading. As long as the two (or more) cells are adjacent—whether they're in a column, row, or both—you can merge them. When you merge two cells, the cell contents are separated by a paragraph mark, as exhibited in Figure 2-2. For instance, by merging cells, you can have a column or row with only one cell. You can then use the larger cell to accommodate long strings of numbers or words.

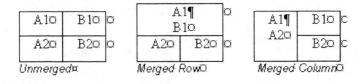

Figure 2-2: *Merging table cells.*

To merge cells:

1. Select adjacent cells.

2. Perform the merge by:
   - right-clicking on the selection and choosing Merge Cells from the shortcut menu;
   - choosing Table→Merge Cells; or
   - using the Merge Cells button on the Tables and Borders toolbar.

ACTIVITY 2-2

Creating a Header Row

Setup: My Driving Directions is open.

Scenario: To identify the table information in My Driving Directions.doc, you decide to add a title to the table. So, you insert a new row at the top of the table and enter the title. However, the title isn't centered over the entire table as you would like it to be. You attempt to center it using the Center alignment button, but are unsuccessful. Finally, you decide to use the merge cell feature to get the affect you need.

While scrolling through the My Driving Directions document, you notice the last row of information is crowed in the first cell. So, you decide to merge the cells of the last row. You then save the file.

What You Do	How You Do It
1. Add a header row at the top of the table.	a. Select the row containing the column headings. (Place the mouse pointer to the left of the row until the mouse pointer becomes a right-pointing arrow and click.) b. Right click and choose Insert Rows.
2. In the new row's first cell, add and center the heading *Driving Directions to Burke*.	a. Click in the new row's first cell, and type *Driving Directions to Burke*. b. Select the new heading. c. On the Standard toolbar, click on the Center Alignment button 🔲 .
3. Is this the affect that you had intended? Can you think of a solution?	
4. Merge the three cells in the first row and center the heading.	a. Select the entire first row. b. From the shortcut menu, choose Merge Cells. c. Use the Center Alignment button to center the heading.
5. Merge the cells in the last row (containing "Once you're nearby...") to create a one-cell row.	a. Select the last row of the table. b. Merge the cells. c. Save and close the file.

TOPIC C

Open an Excel Table in Word

It's likely that you keep some numeric data in Microsoft Excel workbooks. Since you may want to have this data appear in your Word documents, in this topic you will open Excel data in a Word document.

You're writing a letter to a client and find yourself creating a table similar to one that already exists in a Microsoft Excel workbook. Rather than retyping the table data, you can open the Excel data in Word as a Word table.

Open an Excel Table in Word

Procedure Reference   Word allows you to open other Office XP files from Word. For example, you may have table data in a Microsoft Excel workbook that you wish to bring into Word as a Word table. To do this:

1. Display the Open dialog box.

2. From the Files of Type drop-down list box, select All Files (*.*).

3. Double-click on the Excel file.

4. In the Open Worksheet dialog box, select the desired workbook sheets and/or range.

5. Click on OK.

ACTIVITY 2-3

Opening an Excel Table in Word

Objective: Open an Excel Table in Word.

Setup: Word is open with no files open.

Scenario: You need to include a list of current mortgage rates in a memo, named Mortgage Letter.doc, that you are sending to a client. Rather than recreate the wheel, you open an existing list of current mortgage rates that resides in an Excel worksheet named Sort Data.xls as a Word table. You then use the clipboard to move the table to Mortgage Letter.doc. Once the table resides in Mortgage Letter.doc., you save the file as My Mortgage Letter.doc.

What You Do	How You Do It
1. With Mortgage Letter.doc open, display all document file types in the Open dialog box and open the entire workbook file named Sort Rates.xls.	a. **Open** Mortgage Letter.doc.
	b. **Display the Open dialog box.**
	c. **From the Files of Type drop-down list box, select All Files (*.*).**
	d. **Double-click on** Sort Rates.xls.
	e. **Click on OK**
	✎ The Open Worksheet dialog box offers the ability to open only a portion (Sheet or Cell Range) of a Worksheet file.

2. **How is the Excel worksheet data displayed?**

Word Table

3. **Move the entire table to between the body of the letter and the salutation.**	a. **Select the entire table.** (Click on the tables move handle.)
	b. **Place the entire table on the clipboard.**
	c. **In** Mortgage Letter.doc, **position your insertion point before the second return symbol between the body of the letter and the salutation.**
	It·was·a·pleasure·speaking·with·you·today.·As·promised·I·have·included·the·following·table·to·give·you·an·idea·of·the·current·mortgage·rates·in·major·U.S.·cities.·I·hope·that·you·find·it·helpful.·Please·let·me·know·if·I·can·be·of·further·assistance.¶ ¶ ¶ ¶ Sincerely,¶
	d. **Paste the table.**
	e. **Save the file as** My Mortgage Letter.doc.
	f. Close Sort Rates.xls.

TOPIC D

Sort Table Data

As you've seen, tables allow us to organize data making it easier for our audience to absorb it. However, data isn't always entered into tables in the order that we want it to ultimately appear. So, Microsoft Word offers the sorting feature to help you manage your table data. In this topic you will learn how to rearrange table data to meet your needs.

If you are responsible for keeping any Word tables up-to-date, you know how time consuming it can be to enter new table information in an organized order. You first need to identify the correct placement, insert the appropriate number of rows, and then type the new information into the table. Instead, you can enter the new information in rows added to the bottom of the table and then rearrange the data any number of ways using Word's sorting feature.

Sort Table Data

Procedure Reference

Sorting is the act of organizing information in a column according to a specified order. You can sort lists, paragraphs, and tables by text, number, or date. (We'll focus on sorting data in tables.) The big benefit of sorting is that it lets you rearrange data without retyping it.

To sort a series of paragraphs, a list, or a table:

1. Select the item to be sorted.

2. Choose Table→Sort.

3. From the Sort dialog box, set the desired sort options.

4. Click OK.

Sort Order

Typically table sorts are based on the contents of the first column and performed in ascending order, meaning they are sorted from first to last or least to greatest. For example, if you sort a column of last names in ascending order, the names will be sorted alphabetically starting with the letter A. If you sort a column of numbers in ascending order, the numbers go from 0 to 10. You can also sort a list in descending order, which means that the list will go from Z to A, or the numbers from 10 to 0.

 You can also sort on more than one column in a table. For example, if a table contains both last and first name columns, you can sort by last name first, and then by first name second. To do so, use the "Then By" field in the Sort dialog box.

ACTIVITY 2-4

Sorting Table Data

Setup: My Mortgage Letter.doc is open.

Scenario: Now that you have the Excel data displayed in a Word table, you realize that the table data would be more efficient for your client to use if it was sorted in alphabetical order by location. So, you use the sort feature to sort it alphabetically by location. You then save and close the file.

What You Do	How You Do It
1. Sort the table alphabetically by location, being sure to exclude the header row from the sort.	a. Select the entire table.
	b. Choose Table→Sort.
	You can also use the Sort button on the Tables and Borders toolbar to sort table cells.
	c. In the Sort dialog box, under Sort by, **verify that Location, Text, and Ascending are selected..**

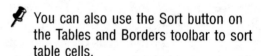

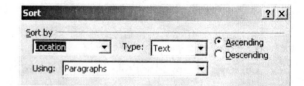

d. Near the bottom of the dialog box, under My List Has, **verify that Header Row is selected.** This will ensure that Word doesn't include the first row of headings in the sort.

e. **Click on OK.** The table is now sorted.

f. **Save and close the file.**

TOPIC E

Perform Calculations in Tables

There may be times when your tables include columns or rows of numeric data that you need to perform calculations on. No need to pull out the calculator because Word can help you out. In this topic you will learn how to perform calculations in tables.

Although you probably keep your large and complex numeric data in Excel workbooks, there may be times when your Word tables include numeric data. For example, you have a table of yearly principle payments over four years and you want to add these numbers to calculate the total principle paid. When this is true, you can calculate those columns or rows using Word's formula feature. By entering formulas in Word, you can change numeric data and then have Word calculate for you.

Formulas

Word has the ability to perform basic calculations in tables.

Formulas are mathematical equations that perform calculations. Table 2-1 shows some samples of Word calculations and their formula examples. These examples use cell references that are identified in Figure 2-3, where letters represent columns and numbers represent rows.

Table 2-1: *Calculations and Formula Examples*

Calculation	Formula Example
Addition	=B2 + C2 or =SUM(B2:C2)
Subtraction	=B2 - C2
Multiplication	=B2 * C2 or =PRODUCT(B2, C2)
Division	=C4 / D4
Average	=AVERAGE(B2, C2, D2)
Percentage	=C2 / 100 then choose a percentage number format, such as 0.00%

 If a table column or row contain blanks cells, you must enter a zero in each blank cell in order for Word to calculate the column or row.

	A	B	C
1	A1	B1	C1
2	A2	B2	C2
3	A3	B3	C3

Figure 2-3: *Cell reference in Word tables.*

Some formulas are composed of functions, like SUM and AVERAGE. For a complete listing of available word functions, choose Tables→Formula and display the Paste Function drop-down list. Note that not all Word calculations have to have functions in their formulas. For instance, neither division nor subtraction has a function. Instead, between cell references, you can just use the minus sign (-) for subtraction and the front slash (/) for division.

When including cell references in a calculation, the cells don't have to be adjacent to one another. To use individual cells in a calculation, just separate the cell references by a comma (A1, B6, C2). To include a range of adjacent cells in a calculation, rather than type each cell reference, use a colon to separate the first cell reference from the last cell reference of the range you want to calculate.

Perform Calculations in Tables

Procedure Reference

Now that you know what formulas are, you're ready to use them. To perform a calculation in a Word table:

1. Place the insertion point in the cell that will contain the calculation result.

2. Choose Table→Formula.

3. Enter the formula, including the function and cell references.

4. If desired, choose a number format.

5. Click OK.

Repeating a Calculation

Some calculations can get pretty involved, so once you've created a calculation with just the right formula, you won't want to re-enter it again. To repeat a calculation, press [F4]. Since it performs the last action again, it's a quick way to repeat formulas in a table. For example, after summing the numbers in one column, simply reposition the insertion point below the next column of numbers and press [F4] to sum those numbers.

The SUM Function

The SUM function is based on the following rules:

- The SUM total's number format will be the same as the numbers used in the calculation.

- The contents of the cell that contains the formula aren't used in the calculation.

- Word first looks for a number above the cell containing the insertion point in order to add up the column. The Formula box will contain: =SUM(ABOVE). If there aren't any numbers directly above the cell with the insertion point, Word will attempt to calculate the sum of the row; the Formula box will contain: =SUM(LEFT).

- The calculation is performed in a specific order, beginning with the cell closest to the cell with the formula and continuing until it reaches either a blank cell or a cell that contains text.

✐ Though the AutoSum button ⬚ located on the Tables and Borders toolbar can quickly calculate sums, it may give you fixed results, like getting SUM(ABOVE) when you want SUM(LEFT). Using the AutoSum button doesn't give you the opportunity to select a number format.

ACTIVITY 2-5

Performing Calculations in Tables

Scenario: You have a document called Loan.doc that contains a table with figures that you need to total. Specifically, you want to total the principal and interest paid columns. Rather than use your calculator to compute the totals and then manually enter them, you decide to use Word's formula feature. To save time, once you create the formula for the principal column, you use the [F4] key to repeat the formula for the interest column. Finally, you save the file as My Loan.doc.

	Principal	Interest	Annual Total
First Year	$2,457.09	$551.20	$3,008.29
Second Year	$2,661.02	$357.27	$3,018.29
Third Year	$2,881.89	$183.40	$3,065.29
Total Paid	$8,000.00	$1,091.87	$9,091.87

Figure 2-4: *The Completed Table*

What You Do	How You Do It
1. In Loan.doc, **position the insertion point in cell B5 and display the Formula dialog box.** You can refer to Figure 2-3 for help on cell references, like B5.	a. **Open** Loan.doc b. **Place the insertion point in the last cell in the Principal column.** c. **Choose Table, Formula.**

2. **Make the necessary setting changes so that your Formula dialog box matches the graphic below and then apply the formula.**	a. **Verify that the Formula box contains =SUM(ABOVE)** in order to calculate the sum of the numbers above the selected cell.
	
	b. **From the Numbers Format drop-down list, select $#,##0.00;($#,##0.00) (the third choice in the list).**
	
	    Applying a number format is not a necessary step in creating formulas, however, it is good practice to get into in case your numbers are unformatted.
	
	c. **Click on OK.**
	
	    The sum should equal $8,000.00.

Formula ?|x|

Formula:
=SUM(ABOVE)

Number format:
$#,##0.00;($#,##0.00)

Paste function: Paste bookmark:

OK   Cancel

Don't do anything between steps 2 and 3. To use the repeat function successfully in step 3, no intermediate tasks can be performed.

3. Use the repeat function to repeat the formula for the interest column.

   a. Position the insertion point in cell C5.

   b. Press the [F4] key.

     🖈 The sum should equal $1,091.87.

4. In cell D2, create a formula that will total the principal and interest paid over the first year and then repeat that formula for the remaining annual totals.

   a. Position the insertion point in cell D2.

   b. Display the Formula dialog box.

   c. Verify that the Formula is =SUM(LEFT).

   d. From the Number Format drop-down list, select the third number format.

   e. Click OK.

   f. Use the repeat function to create formulas for the remaining annual totals.

   g. Save the file as My Loan.doc.

5. Refer to Figure 2-4 to verify your totals.

🖈 Unlike a workbook in Microsoft Excel, Word tables do not update automatically if changes occur in the data. To update any calculations, you will have to select the cell that contains the formula and press [F9].

🖈 To perform complex calculations in tables, consider using Microsoft Excel.

TOPIC F

Create and Modify a Chart Based on Word Table Data

Although tables do a great job of simplifying data, there may be times when a graph or chart would do a better job of communicating the data. Another means of manipulating table data is to use Microsoft Word's charting feature to convert table data to charts. In this topic you will learn the procedure for creating a chart based on Word table data.

The saying "a picture is worth a thousand words" is especially applicable when it comes to table data and charts. Rather than have your audience digest rows and columns of data, why not assist them by displaying the table data in a graph. Charts also work well when presenting numeric data to an audience. Simply put, charts do a great job of simplifying numbers!

Create and Modify a Chart Based on Word Table Data

Procedure Reference

To build charts, Word teams up with another program that's included with Microsoft Office 2002, called Microsoft Graph. With several types to choose from, Microsoft Graph charts are helpful for presenting statistical relationships visually. Each chart is accompanied by its own datasheet, which is a series of columns and rows, similar to a Word table or spreadsheet. The datasheet, because it's linked to a chart, automatically updates the chart as you add, change, or exclude data. You can enter data directly into the datasheet, however, in this topic you will create a chart based on existing Word table data. Figure 2-5 displays the various screen elements when using Microsoft Graph.

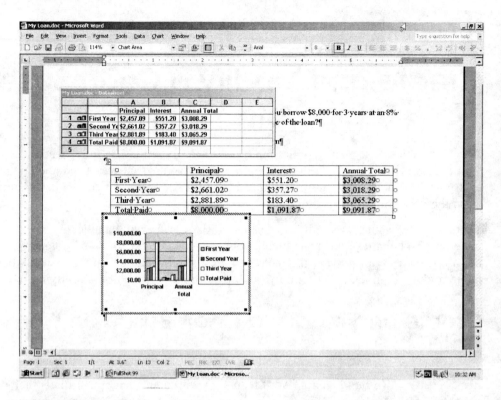

Figure 2-5: *A chart, a datasheet, and the graph, including Microsoft Graph menus and toolbar.*

To create a chart using existing Word table data:

1. Select the table data that you wish to chart, either a portion of the table or the entire table.

2. Choose Insert→Picture→Chart.

3. Include or edit any table data in the datasheet as needed.

4. To return to Word, just click outside of the datasheet or outside of the chart. (To return to Microsoft Graph, just double-click on the chart.)

 To create a new chart with sample data already provided for you, place your insertion point where you want the chart to appear and then follow steps 2–4 above.

Excluding Data from a Chart

There may be times when you want to hide a particular column or row of data in an existing chart because it distracts from the story you're trying to tell. Excluding data from a chart is a way to control which data is displayed and which isn't. To exclude a row or column, in the datasheet, double-click on the gray heading of the column or row you want to exclude. To include it again, simply double-click the heading again.

Changing the Chart Type

Microsoft Graph offers many options for jazzing up your graphs. Being able to change your chart type is just one of them. To change the chart type, while in Microsoft Graph simply choose Chart→Chart Type, and select the desired chart. When selecting a chart type, keep in mind that each general chart type excels at displaying certain types of numeric data.

Importing Data to Create a Chart

If the data is in a file format other than a Word document, you may be able to import it if it's in one of the following file formats.

- Text Delimited (.txt, .csv)
- Lotus 1-2-3 (.wks, .wk1)
- Microsoft Excel (.xls, .xlw, .xlc)

To import a compatible data file into a chart:

1. Create or open a chart and switch to the datasheet, if necessary.
2. Select the cell where the imported data will begin, usually the upper-left cell on the datasheet.
3. Choose Edit→Import File.
4. Using the Look In drop-down list box, locate the folder that contains the data file you want to import.
5. Select the data's file format from the Files Of Type drop-down list box
6. Double-click on the file you want to import

ACTIVITY 2-6

Creating and Modifying a Chart Based on Word Table Data

Setup: My Loan is open.

Scenario: Now that you have your column and row data totaled in the My Loan.doc document, your manager requests a chart that displays the yearly principle and interest table data. You've heard that Word can create charts from table data, so you forge ahead. Once you create the datasheet and chart, you realize that you inadvertently added the total data, so you edit the datasheet to exclude all totals from your chart. To jazz up your chart you decide to experiment with the available chart types in Microsoft Graph. When finished you save and close the file.

The Cost of Borrowing

You want to take out a home improvement loan. If you borrow $8,000 for 3 years at an 8% fixed rate, how much interest will you pay over the life of the loan?

The Estimated Cost of Your Home Improvement Loan
(Principal & Interest Paid by Year)

	Principal	Interest	Annual Total
First Year	$2,457.09	$551.20	$3,008.29
Second Year	$2,661.02	$357.27	$3,018.29
Third Year	$2,881.89	$183.40	$3,065.29
Total Paid	$8,000.00	$1,091.87	$9,091.87

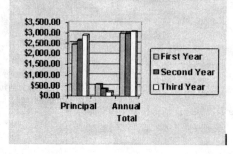

Figure 2-6: *The Completed Chart and Table.*

What You Do	How You Do It
1. Select the table and create a chart.	a. Select the table.
	b. Choose Insert→Picture.

Word offers many options for inserting pictures into documents. You will cover many of them in Lesson 3, but for now we will concentrate on Charts.

c. Choose Chart.

2. What elements are on your screen?

💣 Don't click off of the datasheet, as doing so will close the datasheet and Microsoft Graph. To return to Microsoft Graph, simply double-click on the chart.

3. **Exclude the total columns** so that they don't appear in your chart.

   a. While observing the screen, in the datasheet **double-click on the column heading for column C.** The annual total data is excluded from the chart.

   b. While observing the screen, in the datasheet **double-click on the row heading for row 4.** The total paid data is excluded from the chart.

4. **Display the Chart Type dialog box and apply a clustered column chart with a 3-D visual effect.**

   a. **Choose Chart→Chart Type.**

   b. If necessary, **select the Clustered column with a 3-D visual effect chart type.** (The first chart in the second row.)

   c. **Click OK.**

5. **Close the datasheet.**

   a. **Click outside of the datasheet and away from the chart.**

    You can also use the datasheet close box.

   b. **Save and close the file.**

TOPIC G

Link Excel Data in a Word Table

You now know how to create charts using Word table data. Though, if you're like most business people, you keep much of your numeric table data in Excel worksheets. As you've already seen, Word allows you to open your Excel table data in Word, which eliminates the need to retype the data. You can then chart the data the same way you charted Word table data. But what if you want to ensure that future updates made to the Excel data will occur automatically in the Word document? In this topic you will learn how to connect the two.

Suppose you have figures in an Excel worksheet that you wish to chart in a Word table. The Excel data is dynamic in that you update it frequently. Rather than opening the Excel data in Word, you want to create a link so that future updates made to the Excel data will occur automatically in the Word document. Word can handle this by creating a link between the two files.

Link vs. Embed

As you know, you can duplicate data between Office documents using the copy/paste or collect/paste techniques; the copied information is simply recreated when it's pasted. These techniques for inserting information are fine, but there are two other ways to share data between applications—linking and embedding.

Before you create a *linked object*, you need a source file and a destination file. The source file is where the data is stored and updated, such as an Excel worksheet. The destination file is where the link representing the source file data will be inserted, such as a Word document. Therefore, a linked object is an object that is created in a source file and inserted into a destination file, while maintaining a connection between the two files. A linked object in the destination file can be updated when the source file is updated.

Embedding Objects

If you have only temporary or infrequent access to a source file or if you don't need to update the information very often, linking may not be the best option. For instance, suppose you're on the road using your laptop to show a client your annual report, which is a Word document, and you suddenly realize that the document is linked to an Excel worksheet that's stored on the network back at the office? Your links would be broken, meaning that if you tried to open the source file, you'd get an error message. How could you have access to that information without linking to it? You could embed the Excel information (the object) in your Word document.

Unlike creating a link, creating an *embedded object* stores the object directly in the destination file—without any link to the source file. Consequently, changes made to the source file will not affect the embedded object—there's no link.

Although embedding doesn't link to a source file, it does provide access to the embedded object's original application menus and toolbars within the destination file's program. For instance, say you embedded an Excel Worksheet Object in a Word document. When you edit the embedded Excel object, you'll notice that the Word menus and toolbars are replaced by Excel menus and toolbars—even though Word is the active application!

Link Excel Data in a Word Table

Creating a Linked Object

If you have data that is updated frequently and needs to be in two places at the same time, then inserting a link between the two files is for you. The easiest way to create a link between the source file and the destination file is to:

1. Position your insertion point in the document where you want to add the link.

2. Choose Insert→Object.

3. In the Object dialog box, select the Create From File tab.

4. Select the Link To File check box.

5. Use the Browse button to find the object.

6. Click OK.

 If you double-click on a linked object, the originating application opens and loads the data from the linked external file.

Embedding an Object

The procedure for embedding an object is similar to the linking process, except rather than selecting Paste in step 3, you just select Paste Special. To embed an object:

1. Position your insertion point in the document where you want to embed the object.

2. Choose Insert→Object.

3. In the Object dialog box, select the Create New tab.

4. In the Object Type box, select the type of object that you want to insert.

5. Click OK.

 If you double-click on an embedded object, the originating applications menus and toolbars replace the Word equivalents, even though you're still working in Word.

Linked Data

The linked object in the destination file is displayed merely as a copy of the source data. Now any time the source data are updated, the linked object in the destination file will also be updated.

Since the data is not actually stored in the destination file, if you double-click on the linked object, it acts as a shortcut to the source file—opening the source file and its application, if necessary.

ACTIVITY 2-7

Linking Excel Data in a Word Table

Setup: Word is open with no files open.

Scenario: You have a document named Marketing Piece.doc (the destination file) that you want to link to an Excel worksheet file named Company Results.xls (the source file). You begin by opening the destination file and adding some explanatory text to it. You then use the Insert command to create the link. To test the link, you edit the source file. You save the file as My Marketing Piece.doc and close the file, and close Microsoft Excel.

What You Do	How You Do It
1. In Marketing Piece.doc, **add the following sentence as a new paragraph at the end of the document, including two returns after the sentence.** *Our Philadelphia sales numbers speak for themselves:*	a. **Open** Marketing Piece.doc. b. At the end of the document, **type** *Our Philadelphia sales numbers speak for themselves:.* c. **Press [Enter] twice.**
2. **Use the Insert→Object command to create a link to** Company Results.xls.	a. **Choose Insert→Object.** b. **Select the Create From File tab.** c. **Check the Link To File box.** d. **Click Browse and double-click on Company Results.xls.**

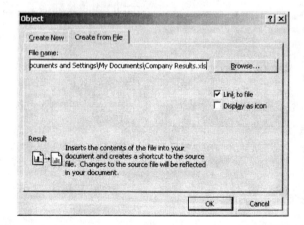

e. **Click OK.** The linked object is inserted into the Word document.

3. Now that the link exists, let's make an edit to the source file directly from Word. **Use the linked objects shortcut menu to display the source file and edit cell B7 to *204*.**

   a. **Right-click on the linked object (the Excel table).**

   b. **Choose Linked Worksheet Object→Edit Link.** Since the source file was already opened in Excel, your computer just switches to the source file.

   c. **Click in cell B7 and type *204* and press [Enter]** to edit the cell contents.

4. **Verify that the edit occurred in the Word table.**

   a. **In the taskbar, select the Word button.**

   b. **Observe the table.** The link works!

   c. **Save the file as My Marketing Piece, and then close the file.**

   d. **Close Microsoft Excel, without saving changes.**

Lesson 2 Follow-up

In this lesson you went beyond the basics of creating simple tables and learned to use Word's intermediate table features including converting existing tabbed text into a table, merging table cells, sorting table data, performing calculations in tables, creating charts based on table data, and how to link documents between applications.

1. **Of the table features included in this lesson, which ones will you implement in your tables at work?**

2. **When might you link an Excel workbook to a Word document.**

NOTES

LESSON 3
Adding Graphics

Data Files:
Burke Flyer.doc

Lesson Time:
30–40 minutes

Lesson Objectives:

In this lesson, you will learn how to insert, manipulate, and format graphic images, including clip art, AutoShapes, WordArt, and organization charts.

You will:

- insert a clip art image by using the Media Gallery.
- insert a pre-formatted shape and change its fill color.
- create a WordArt graphic.
- create an organization chart.

Introduction

So far, you've been working with text-based documents. However, all text and no pictures makes a dull document. In this lesson, you'll gain some hands-on experience converting a basic text document into a lively and colorful flyer, so that you can do the same for your own brochures or newsletters.

In the "good-old days" working with art meant carefully clipping art out of clip art books and pasting the art onto layout boards. Consequently, artwork was often left in the hands of a professional graphic designer. However, with today's computers and word processing programs, it doesn't take much to spice up a document with a colorful title or a cool graphic.

TOPIC A

Insert a Clip Art Image

There are all kinds of pictures you can add to a document, but a great starting place is the wide selection of pictures that are included on the Microsoft Office CD-ROM. That's where you will start in this lesson.

As everything becomes more Web-oriented and geared for visual impact, graphics play an even more crucial role in your work. Don't worry if you're not an artist, instead of creating your own drawings, you can take advantage of Microsoft's treasure chest of pictures. Using artwork that has already been created, it's easy to add graphics to your documents, and the results are nothing short of professional!

What is a Graphic?

A *graphic* is an image that illustrates, compliments, or calls attention to your text. In Microsoft Word and the other applications that are part of the Microsoft Office suite, there are two general types of graphics you can add:

*   *Pictures*: These are graphics such as bitmaps, scanned pictures and photographs, and clip art, which are stored in another file.
*   *Drawing objects*: These are graphics such as curves, lines, AutoShapes, WordArt drawing objects, and diagrams that you draw or insert. These objects are part of your Word document.

    A document can include many types of graphics, including pictures and drawn objects. The document for this lesson will include WordArt, clip art, a diagram, and an AutoShape.

Clip Art

You will begin by working with pictures, specifically clip art; later in the lesson you will work with drawing objects.

Definition: Microsoft Word provides a selection of pictures, or *clip art,* that you can use in your documents. These are professionally designed and created images that ship with Microsoft Office in the *Clip Organizer*—a gallery of drawings, photographs, sounds, videos, and other media files that you can use in your documents.

When you install Word, some pictures are loaded onto your hard disk. The Microsoft Office CD-ROM contains additional graphics you can use.

Example: There are hundreds of clip art graphics you can choose from. You will find pictures of animals, people, buildings, business, food, household, leisure, nature, sciences, sports, technology, travel, vehicles, and so on. There are also decorative elements such as backgrounds, borders, and frames. Clip art images are grouped into categories so they are easier to locate. Figure 3-1 shows some clip art images you'll find in the Clip Organizer.

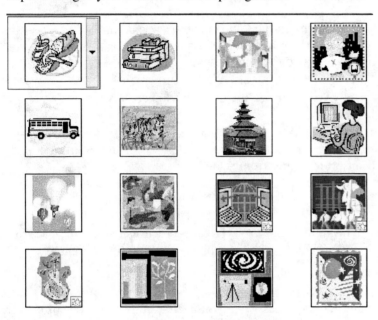

Figure 3-1: *Word offers a wide variety of clip art images.*

Insert a Clip Art Image

Procedure Reference To insert a clip art image in your document:

1. Place the insertion point where you want the piece of clip art to be placed.

2. Display the Insert Clip Art task pane by:
   - Choosing Insert→Picture→Clip Art.
   - Click the Insert Clip Art button on the Drawing toolbar.

3. Set your search criteria.
   - In the Search text box, type a word or phrase that describes the clip you want or type in all or some of the file name of the clip. You can use normal, everyday language.
   - By default, Word will search the entire Clip Organizer. If you want to narrow your search, you can specify the clip collections you want to search or ignore.
   - By default, Word will search for all media types, including clip art, photographs, movies, and sounds. You can choose to search only for certain types of media files.

4. Click Search.

5. Once you find the clip you want to insert, click on it to insert it.

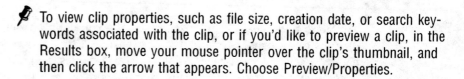 To view clip properties, such as file size, creation date, or search keywords associated with the clip, or if you'd like to preview a clip, in the Results box, move your mouse pointer over the clip's thumbnail, and then click the arrow that appears. Choose Preview/Properties.

6. Close the Insert Clip Art task pane.

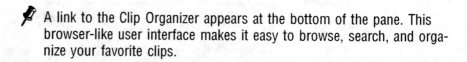 A link to the Clip Organizer appears at the bottom of the pane. This browser-like user interface makes it easy to browse, search, and organize your favorite clips.

7. Move and resize the graphic as necessary.

Inserting a Picture from a File

If Word doesn't have what you're looking for, don't worry—you can use existing pictures from another source. This is called inserting a picture from a file. To insert a picture from a file:

1. Choose Insert→Picture→From File.
2. Move to the folder containing the graphics file you want to insert.
3. From the Files Of Type drop-down list, select the picture's file format. Word can insert most popular graphic file formats.
4. Double-click on the file you want to insert.

Online Clips

There may be times when you need a particular piece of clip art that's unavailable in the Clip Organizer. If you have an Internet connection and Web browser, you can use the *Microsoft Design Gallery Live* on the Web to find more clip art. At this site, you can browse Microsoft's collection of images and download them for free. To access the online clip art, click on the Clips Online link in the Insert Clip Art task pane.

 If you use a clip other than what's provided by Microsoft or created by you, make sure that you have permission to use it.

Move, Size, and Delete Graphics

Once you've put a graphic in your document, you're probably not done working with it. Chances are, it isn't exactly the size or in the position you want. You can move, resize, and even delete graphics to make your documents more appealing. Table 3-1 lists some ways you can manipulate your graphics.

Table 3-1: *Manipulating a Graphic*

To:	Procedure:
Select a graphic	Click on the graphic once. Selection handles appear around the graphic and the Picture toolbar opens. You can use the buttons on the Picture toolbar to work with your graphic.

To:	Procedure:
Change the size of a graphic	1. Select the graphic.
	2. Position the mouse pointer over one of the sizing handles.
	3. Drag the sizing handle until the object is the shape and size you want.
	Tips:
	• Use any of the corner selection handles to size the graphic proportionately.
	• If you want to keep the center of the object in the same place, hold down [Ctrl] while dragging the mouse.
	• To maintain the object's proportions, hold down [Shift] while dragging the mouse.
	To specify precise measurements, double-click the graphic. In the Format Picture dialog box, select the Size tab. In the Height and Width boxes, enter the measurements and then click OK.
Move a graphic	1. Select the graphic.
	2. Drag the graphic to its new location.
	Tips:
	• To constrain an object so it moves only horizontally or vertically, press [Shift] as you drag the object.
	• To nudge an object in small increments, press the arrow keys.
	• To move a graphic to a new location in the document, use the Cut and Paste buttons.
Delete a graphic	Select the graphic and press [Delete].

ACTIVITY 3-1

Inserting a Clip Art Image

Setup: Word is open with no files open.

Scenario: You've prepared the text for the Burke Flyer.doc, an informational piece that describes your services to potential clients. To jazz it up a bit, you're going to add some graphics. To begin, you need to find and insert clip art—it only makes sense that you'll search first for a picture of a house, which you will insert before the heading "Make Burke Properties Your Realtor." Once you've inserted the clip art, you decide to size and move it so that it fits in better with the other text in the document. You save the file as My Burke Flyer.doc. Finally, you close the Insert Clip Art task pane.

What You Do	How You Do It
1. With the Burke Flyer.doc open, display the Clip Art task pane.	a. **Open** Burke Flyer.doc.
	b. **Position the insertion point is in front of the "M" in the heading "Make Burke Properties Your Realtor."**
	c. **Choose Insert→Picture→Clip Art.**
2. Search for a picture of a house, narrowing your search to exclude Web collections.	a. In the Search text box in the Insert Clip Art task pane, **type** *house*.
	b. In the Insert Clip Art task pane under Other Search Options, **click on the Search In drop-down arrow.**
	c. From the drop-down list, **uncheck Web Collections.**
	d. **Click on the drop-down arrow.** The Search In drop-down list box displays Selected Collections.
3. Insert the first clip art from the search results and close the Insert Clip Art task pane.	a. **Click Search** to start the search. The Insert Clip Art task pane displays the results by listing thumbnails of drawings, photos, sounds, and other media files.
	b. **Click on the first clip art image** to insert the image in your document.
	c. **Close the Insert Clip Art task pane.**

4. Size the house picture so that it is smaller, but still proportionate.

    a. **Click once on the picture** to select it. Small black selection handles around the graphic indicate that you have selected it.

    b. **Move the mouse pointer over the bottom-right corner handle until it becomes a two-headed arrow.** The arrow will change to a crosshair when you start resizing the picture.

    c. **Press [Shift] and drag the mouse pointer up and to the left to approximately the 2 1/4" mark on the horizontal ruler.**

5. Move the house picture to the right side of the document; save the document.

    a. **Point to the middle of the graphic.** The mouse pointer becomes a four-headed arrow.

    b. **Drag the image to right side of the document.**

    c. When the image is at the right margin, **release the mouse pointer.**

    d. **Click outside of the image** to see how the image looks in its new location.

    e. **Save the file as *My Burke Flyer*.**

TOPIC B

Add an AutoShape

Sometimes you just need a simple shape, like an arrow, a circle, or a box. In addition to inserting pictures, Word enables you to draw lines and insert shapes in your document. That's what we'll look at in this topic.

If you can't find just the right piece of clip art, or if you need a very customized graphic, the best way to create it is to draw it yourself! With the tools found on the Drawing toolbar, you can make tailor-made flow charts, maps, and other line drawings.

The Drawing Toolbar

The *Drawing toolbar* enables you to draw and format many different kinds of graphics. For example, you can draw regular, dashed, and arrow lines; basic shapes; 3D shapes; and AutoShapes, such as lines, arrows, stars, banners, and callouts.

With the Drawing toolbar, you can enhance graphics—by adding fill color, changing line color and style, and so on—and modify graphics—by changing the line size or line color, or by adding a shadow or 3–D effect. You can also resize, move, rotate, flip, color, and combine shapes.

Figure 3-2: *The Drawing toolbar.*

For your basic drawing tasks, select the tool from the Drawing toolbar. Then click and drag in the document to create the graphic.

AutoShapes

Definition: AutoShapes are ready-made shapes you can insert into your documents by choosing a shape from the AutoShapes drop-down menu. There are many different types of AutoShapes, including basic shapes, lines, connectors, flowchart symbols, starts, banners, callouts, and other common shapes.

Example: Figure 3-3 shows the AutoShapes you can add to your documents.

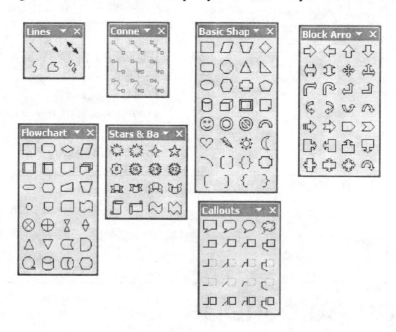

Figure 3-3: *Available AutoShapes.*

Add an AutoShape

Procedure Reference To add an AutoShape to a document:

1. If necessary, display the Drawing toolbar.

2. Click the AutoShapes button on the Drawing toolbar.

3. Point to a category, and then click the desired shape in the submenu that appears.

4. The drawing canvas displays. Point with the crosshair mouse pointer to the upper-left corner of the area where you want to draw the shape, and drag diagonally down and to the right. Release the mouse button to finish drawing the shape.

🖈 To keep lines straight, or to draw a perfectly proportionate shape, such as a square or circle, hold down [Shift] as you drag.

The Drawing Canvas

When you insert an AutoShape in Microsoft Word, a *drawing canvas* is placed around it. The drawing canvas is an area upon which you can draw multiple shapes. When you draw multiples shapes, the drawing canvas helps you arrange and move the shapes. In addition, you can move and resize shapes that are contained within the drawing canvas as a unit. If necessary, you can resize the drawing canvas.

🖈 You can turn the Drawing Canvas on and off by choosing Tools→Options. On the General tab, check or uncheck the Automatically Create Drawing Canvas When Inserting AutoShapes checkbox.

Drawing Layers

As you draw objects in Word, each object is placed in its own individual layer. That is, the first object you draw will be on the layer below the second object you draw. If your objects overlap one another, you can change the order of layers by using the Draw button. For example, you have three objects overlapping each other in a document. You want to change their order by moving the top object to the bottom of the pile. To do so, select the object you want to reorder. On the Drawing toolbar, click the Draw button, select Order, and select Send To Back. Word moves the object to the back of the stack.

ACTIVITY 3-2

Adding an AutoShape

Setup: The document My Burke Flyer is open.

Scenario: To add extra dash to the flyer, you want to create an effect at the bottom that grabs the readers' attention and gets them into your office to meet you or one of the realtors. You'll add an interesting AutoShape to the document and then change its fill color. A sample result is shown in Figure 3-4. Finally, you save the file.

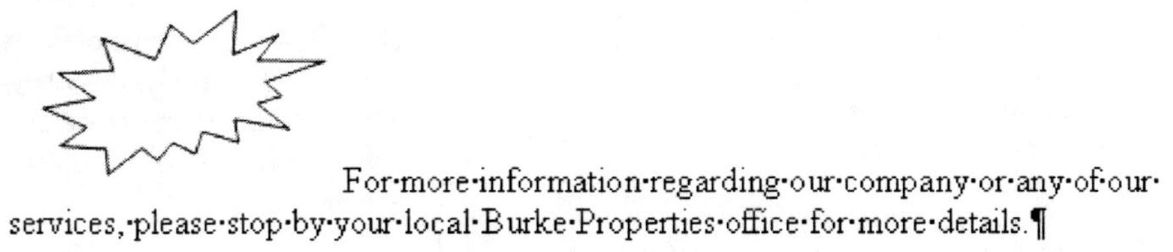

For·more·information·regarding·our·company·or·any·of·our· services,·please·stop·by·your·local·Burke·Properties·office·for·more·details.¶

Figure 3-4: *The completed Autoshape.*

Might have to go to Tools Options General Turn off canvas

What You Do	How You Do It
1. Display and dock the Drawing toolbar.	a. Choose View→Toolbars→Drawing.
	b. If necessary, **drag the Drawing toolbar to the bottom of the window.**
2. At the beginning of the last paragraph, **add an AutoShape of your choice that measures about 1 1/2" width x 1 1/2" height.**	a. **Position the insertion point before the word "For" in the last paragraph.**
	b. On the Drawing toolbar, **click the AutoShapes button** AutoShapes ▾ .
	c. **Choose Stars and Banners.**
	d. **Select an AutoShape you like.**
	e. **Press and hold [Shift]** to prepare to draw a proportionate shape.
	f. Using the ruler as a guide, **click in the upper-left corner of the drawing canvas and then drag the mouse pointer diagonally down and to the right** so that the shape is about 1 1/2 by 1 1/2 inches.
	g. **Release [Shift] and release the mouse button.**
3. Resize the canvas area so that the border fits more closely to the AutoShape.	a. **Position the mouse pointer over the upper-right corner of the drawing canvas** ⌐ The mouse pointer changes to a corner handle.
	b. **Drag the upper-right corner handle to the left to about the 1 1/2 inch marker on the horizontal ruler.**
	c. **Position the mouse pointer over the lower-right corner of the drawing canvas.**
	d. **Drag the corner handle up to about the 1 1/2 inch marker on the vertical ruler.** The canvas area now appears in the document and the text for the paragraph is on a new page.

4. **Specify a fill color of your choice for the AutoShape.**

a. **Click on the AutoShape** to select it.

b. On the Drawing toolbar, **click the down arrow on the Fill Color button** 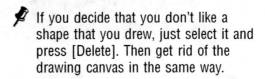 .

c. **Choose a color.** The AutoShape now has the fill color you chose.

d. **Click outside of the drawing canvas.** The drawing canvas boundary disappears.

> If you decide that you don't like a shape that you drew, just select it and press [Delete]. Then get rid of the drawing canvas in the same way.

e. **Save the file.**

TOPIC C

Insert WordArt

When you spice up your document with graphics, you have to work with images that are separate from your text. With WordArt you can add pizazz to the text itself. As you continue with this topic, you'll add headings and titles with a special effect.

You've probably seen advertising with wavy or slanted 3-dimensional headlines. Have you ever wanted to create similar effects in your own Word documents? You can with the WordArt tool. Being aware of all of the possibilities and knowing how to use WordArt will enable you to create unique text effects.

What is WordArt?

Definition: *WordArt WordArt* takes your words and turns them into a work of art. From the WordArt Gallery, you can combine any of 24 different styles with any font you have on your computer to design some amazing graphic effects. WordArt enables you to create shadowed, skewed, rotated, and stretched text as well as text that has been fitted to predefined shapes.

Example: WordArt can be used for headings, logos, and other artistic page elements that incorporate words, as shown here.

Non-Example: Without using WordArt, you can format text to be bold, italic, underline, and outline. While this can be interesting, the end result is not considered WordArt, because the text is not treated as a single object.

Insert WordArt

Procedure Reference To insert a WordArt object:

1. Display the Word Art Gallery by:
   - clicking on the Insert WordArt button [🄰] on the Drawing toolbar; or
   - choosing Insert→Picture→WordArt.

2. Select a style or effect from the WordArt Gallery and click OK.

3. Type the text you want to make into a WordArt object (set font, size, and formatting options, if desired).

4. Click OK.

   🖉 The default font and text size for WordArt is Arial, black, and 36 pt.

WordArt Options Once you've created a WordArt object, you don't have to leave it as is—you can modify it by using the WordArt toolbar.

For example, select a WordArt object and click the Edit Text button to modify the WordArt object's text, font, size, or style. Or, to change a WordArt object's colors and line styles:

1. Select a WordArt object and click the Format WordArt button [🎨].

2. On the Colors and Lines tab in the Format WordArt dialog box, select a fill color, a line color, style, and weight.

3. Click OK.

ACTIVITY 3-3

Inserting WordArt

Setup: The document My Burke Flyer is open.

Scenario: You realize that the perfect place to throw in some WordArt would be the very top of the flyer where you could add the company name. You decide to create a WordArt image that includes the text "Burke Properties." You'll select the look you want to start with and then make a change. You'll then save the file.

What You Do	How You Do It
1. **Insert a WordArt image for Burke Properties at the top of the document.**	a. **Press [Ctrl][Home]** to move the insertion point to the top of the document.
	b. On the Drawing toolbar, **click the Insert WordArt button**  to display the WordArt Gallery.
	c. In the WordArt Gallery dialog box **select the second style in the second row.**

d. **Click OK.**

e. In the text box, **type *Burke Properties*.**

f. **Click OK** to insert the WordArt object into the document.

2. **Change the font of the WordArt to one of your choice.**

a. **Select the WordArt image.**

📌 The WordArt toolbar appears automatically when you click an existing WordArt item in Print Layout view.

b. **On the WordArt toolbar, click the Edit Text button** | Edit Text... | **.**

c. **Change the font to one of your choice.**

d. **Click OK.**

e. **Save the file.**

TOPIC D

Insert an Organizational Chart

We've worked with clip art, AutoShapes, and WordArt. Finally we'll turn our attention to diagrams and charts.

For many people, using diagrams or organization charts is a big part of their working life. If you've ever tried to create an organization chart from scratch, you know how difficult and tedious it can be. After all, there are software applications dedicated just to creating organization charts. As you'll find out in this topic, Word has a built-in feature that enables you to create and customize many different charts and diagrams, including organization charts.

What is an Organization Chart?

You can add a variety of diagrams to your document using the diagramming tools on the Drawing toolbar. The *Diagram Gallery* enables you to add the following types of diagrams to your documents:

- Organization chart: shows hierarchical relationships.
- Cycle diagram: illustrates a process with a continuous cycle.
- Radial diagram: shows relationships of a core element.
- Pyramid diagram: shows foundation-based relationships.
- Venn diagram: illustrates areas of overlap between elements.
- Target diagram: represents steps toward a goal.

Definition: An *organization chart* shows the hierarchical organization of your company or department. The chart itself consists of shapes in which you enter information, such as the names and titles of people in your organization. The location of the shapes in the organization chart and the lines connecting them indicate the levels and relationships of people in the organization. This table defines the shapes you can have in your organization chart.

Shape	Definition
Superior	A shape that appears above and is connected to another shape.
Assistant	A shape that appears below and is connected to another shape with an elbow connector. This shape appears above any other subordinate shapes for the superior shape it is attached to.
Subordinate	A shape that appears below and is connected to a superior shape.
Coworker	A shape that appears next to another shape that is connected to the same superior shape.

Typically, all organization charts will include a set of shapes connected by lines; however the number of shapes and their layout will be unique to each organization.

Example: Figure 3-5 shows a sample organization chart.

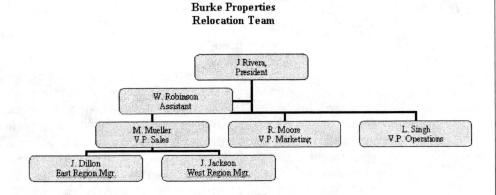

Figure 3-5: *A sample organization chart.*

Insert an Organization Chart

Procedure Reference To create a basic organization chart:

1. Open the Diagram Gallery by:
   - clicking on the Insert Diagram or Organization Chart button [icon] on the Drawing toolbar; or
   - choosing Insert→Picture→Organization Chart.

2.   Select an Organization Chart diagram and click OK.

3.   Inside each shape, type the text you want to include.

Editing an Organiza-tion Chart

As people come and go and times change, you can update your organization chart. Like other drawn objects, you can modify the organization-chart shapes and text. Some changes you might make include adding more shapes, changing branch layout options, and resizing the organization chart. You can also format the organization chart with preset styles, add color, fills, textures or backgrounds, and change the line weight.

To add a shape to an organization chart:

1.   Select the shape you want to add the new shape to. The Organization Chart toolbar opens.

2.   On the Insert Shape button on the Organization Chart toolbar, click the drop-down arrow and choose the shape you want to add.

3.   Enter text in the new shape.

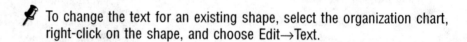 To change the text for an existing shape, select the organization chart, right-click on the shape, and choose Edit→Text.

If you find that your organization chart is so large it threatens to take over your document, you can resize it to fit the contents of your document. To do so, on the Organization Chart toolbar, choose Layout→Fit Organization Chart To Contents.

ACTIVITY 3-4

Inserting an Organization Chart

Setup: My Burke Flyer.doc is open.

Scenario: In one section of the flyer you describe how the company organization is growing. What a perfect place to include a concise organization chart, outlining how you all fit together. You commit a slight oversight, though, and neglect to include the office assistant. It just so happens that Molly is the first face many of your clients will see or talk to, so you add a shape to the organization chart . The resulting chart seems a bit large, so you opt to fit it to the contents of the report. You should be all set at that point! When you're finished, your organization chart should look like Figure 3-5. Finally you save the file.

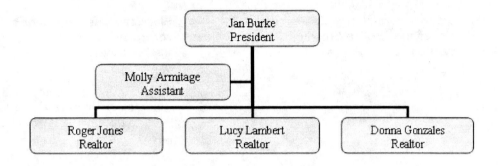

Figure 3-6: *The completed organizational chart.*

What You Do	How You Do It
1. Insert a default organization chart under the "We're Growing" section.	a. Place the insertion point before the return symbol below the "We're Growing" section.

b. On the Drawing toolbar, **click the Insert Diagram Or Organization Chart button** to display the Diagram Gallery dialog box.

c. **Click OK** to insert an organization chart in the document. The Organization Chart toolbar opens and the organization chart appears in the document with drawing space around it, outlined by a nonprinting border and sizing handles.

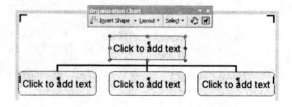

2. **Add text to the organization chart; include names and titles for Burke Property employees as shown in** Figure 3-5

   a. Click inside the top shape and type *Jan Burke* press [Enter] and type *President* .

   b. In the second row of shapes, **click inside the shape on the left and type** *Roger Jones* **press [Enter] and type** *Realtor.*

   c. **In the remaining boxes, enter the following employees:** *Lucy Lambert, Realtor. Donna Gonzales, Realtor.*

   d. **Click away from the organization chart** to deselect it.

3. **Add an assistant, Molly Armitage, to the company president.**

   a. **Select the shape for Jan Burke.**

   b. On the Organization Chart toolbar, **click on the Insert Shape drop-down arrow and choose Assistant.**

   c. **Add the name** *Molly Armitage* **and her title** *Assistant* **to the new shape.**

4. Fit the organization chart to the contents of your document; then save and close the file.

a. Select the shape for Jan Burke.

b. On the Organization Chart toolbar, click the Layout button.

c. From the drop-down list, select Fit Organization Chart to Contents.

d. Scroll up to see the results of adding an organization chart.

e. Scroll through the entire document to see all of the graphics you've added.

f. Save and close the file.

Lesson 3 Follow-up

You've exercised your artistic energies and learned about different types of graphics that you can add to your document. In this lesson, you tried your hand at inserting and manipulating clip art, AutoShapes, WordArt, and organization charts. You've got what it takes to get started putting graphics to work in your document for visual impact and effectiveness.

1. Which types of graphics will you use most in your work? For instance, do you have a particular need for creating organization charts or WordArt?

2. What categories of clip art do you anticipate to be most useful to you?

LESSON 4
Creating a Newsletter

Data Files:
Newsletter Layout.doc
Newsletter Text.doc

Lesson Time:
40–50 minutes

Lesson Objectives:

In this lesson, you will create a newsletter using columns, sections, and graphics.

You will:

- create and format a document section.
- convert existing tabbed text into newsletter columns.
- add column breaks to control the flow of text in newsletter columns.
- wrap text around a graphic.
- create an envelope and mailing label and review the procedure for printing them.

LESSON 4

Introduction

In the previous lessons you created styles and templates, managed table data, and added graphics to documents. With these new skills, and the skills that you brought with you to class, you are ready to create a newsletter. Newsletter are a good way to communicate information to employees, current customers, or potential customers. In this lesson you will create a quarterly newsletter complete with columns, tables, and graphic data.

Many organizations use newsletters to keep clients and employees up-to-date on their organization's progress. You can create exciting and easy to read newsletters using Word's newsletter column tool.

TOPIC A

Create a Document Section

Because you will want to be able to format areas of your newsletter differently, in this topic you will learn how to section off areas of documents so that you can apply formats specific to that area's needs, without effecting the formatting of the rest of the document.

Newsletters can contain separate areas of text, like headings, subheadings, tables, graphics, or boxes containing shaded areas of text, to name just a few. Because you may want to apply different formatting to each of these areas, Word offers the sections feature for setting them apart from each other. Once you separate areas into sections, you can then apply margin, alignment, or page orientation settings, for example, to each separate section without affecting the formatting of other sections within the document.

Sections

Definition: When you create a new document, it is made up of just one *section*, though not every document has to have only one section. If you want to apply different sets of formatting to multiple areas of a document you will want to use sections. A section is a portion of a document that can have unique page formatting options that are separate from the surrounding document, thereby allowing you to vary page setup features within a document. A section can be as small as a single paragraph. The following list presents the major formatting options that can vary from section to section:

- features that you set using the Page Setup dialog box, like margins, paper orientation, paper size; and vertical alignment;

- headers and footers, including page numbering;

- the number of columns; or

- page borders

Example: If you've ever seen a magazine article where the title of an article was positioned over two columns of text, then you've seen what can be done with sections. In this case the article title is one section, and the two columns of text is another section.

Inserting Section Breaks

In order to create a section, you must insert a *section break.* A section break is a nonprinting double line you insert when you want to create a new section. Although documents can have as many section breaks as you want, too many sections can be difficult to manage. Note that a section break mark stores the formatting features of the contents directly above the break. Sections breaks are marked on-screen in various ways depending on which type of section break it is, and which View you are in. All section breaks are visible in Normal View. Table 4-1 lists the four available section break types and their descriptions.

Table 4-1: *Section Break Types*

Section Type:	Description:
Next page	Starts the following section's text at the beginning of a new page.
Continuous	Starts the following section's text immediately following the text in the previous section, with no line or page breaks, unless the two sections have different settings for page size or orientation. In those cases, the new section will be on a new page even if you select this option.
Even Page	Starts the following section's text at the beginning of the next even-numbered page. If the next page is odd-numbered, a blank page is inserted.
Odd Page	Starts the following section's text at the beginning of the next odd-numbered page. If the next page is odd-numbered, a blank page is inserted.

 To delete a section break, switch to Normal view and select the section-break mark and press Delete. Once you delete a section break, that section's contents are joined with the following section and assume that section's formatting.

Word's Views

Word offers four view types for viewing documents.

- Print Layout view—the default view, allows you to see how text, graphics, and other elements will be positioned on the printed page.

- Web Layout view—is used for creating a Web page or a document that is viewed on screen. This view simulates a Web browser.

- Normal view—simplifies page layout so that you can type and edit quickly. It doesn't display headers, footers, backgrounds, drawing objects, or pictures.

- Outline view—useful for long, structured documents where you may wish to move, copy, and reorganize text by dragging headings.You can switch between views using the buttons just above the status bar on the left of the screen or by selecting from the View menu.

Create a Document Section

Procedure Reference   To create a new section:

1. Place the insertion point where you want the new section to end.

2. Choose Insert→Break.

3. From the Section Breaks area, select the type of break you want to insert.

4. Click OK.

ACTIVITY 4-1

Creating a Document Section

Setup: Word is open.

Scenario: Your manager has asked you to create a quarterly newsletter that keeps clients and employees up-to-date on the company's latest happenings. You will use two files—Newsletter Layout.doc, which contains some general layout data, and Newsletter Text.doc which contains the body text for the newsletter. In Newsletter Layout.doc, you insert continuous section breaks, and apply page set up formatting to the heading section. Finally, you save the file as My Newsletter Layout.doc.

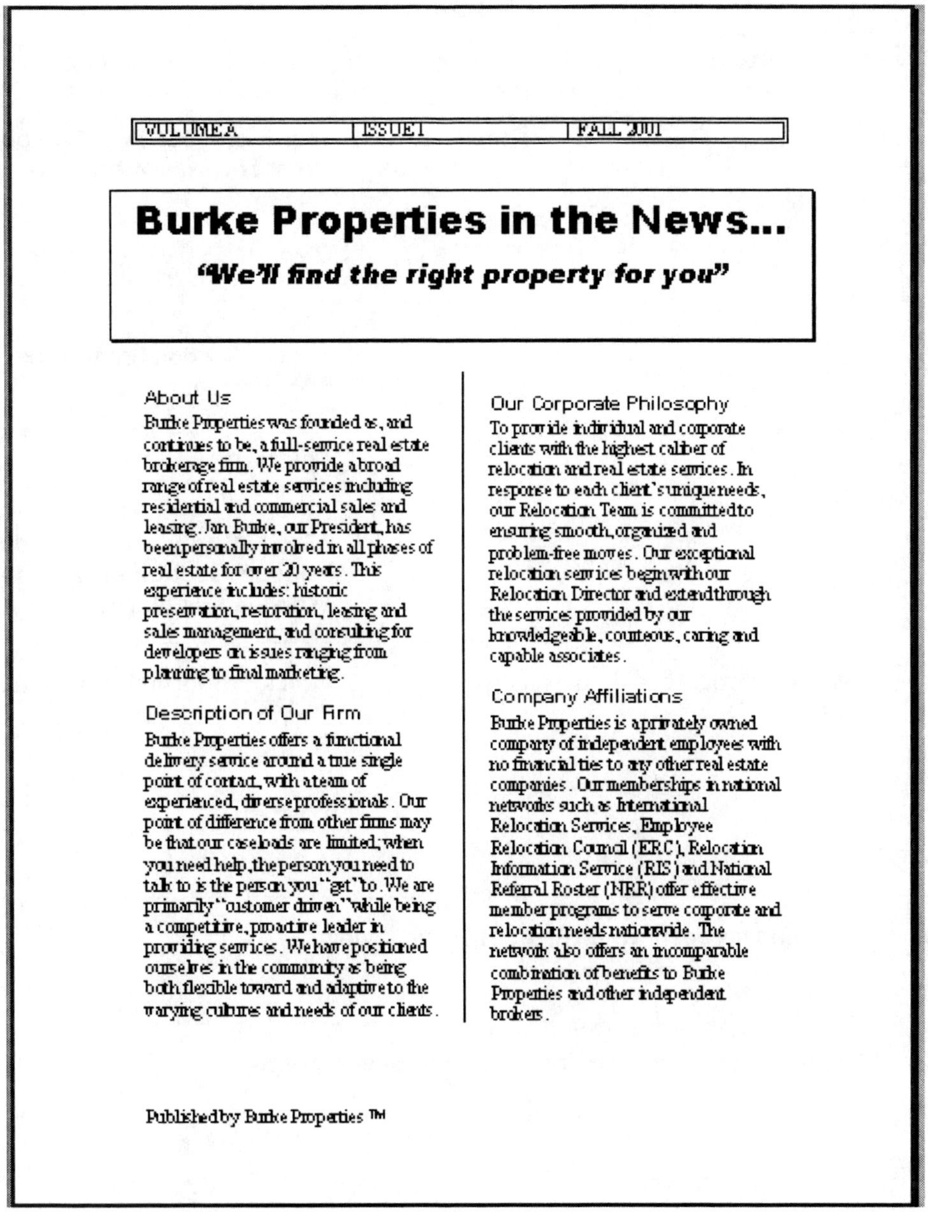

VOLUME A	ISSUE 1	FALL 2001

Burke Properties in the News...

"We'll find the right property for you"

About Us

Burke Properties was founded as, and continues to be, a full-service real estate brokerage firm. We provide a broad range of real estate services including residential and commercial sales and leasing. Jan Burke, our President, has been personally involved in all phases of real estate for over 20 years. This experience includes: historic preservation, restoration, leasing and sales management, and consulting for developers on issues ranging from planning to final marketing.

Description of Our Firm

Burke Properties offers a functional delivery service around a true single point of contact, with a team of experienced, diverse professionals. Our point of difference from other firms may be that our caseloads are limited; when you need help, the person you need to talk to is the person you "get" to. We are primarily "customer driven" while being a competitive, proactive leader in providing services. We have positioned ourselves in the community as being both flexible toward and adaptive to the varying cultures and needs of our clients.

Our Corporate Philosophy

To provide individual and corporate clients with the highest caliber of relocation and real estate services. In response to each client's unique needs, our Relocation Team is committed to ensuring smooth, organized and problem-free moves. Our exceptional relocation services begin with our Relocation Director and extend through the services provided by our knowledgeable, courteous, caring and capable associates.

Company Affiliations

Burke Properties is a privately owned company of independent employees with no financial ties to any other real estate companies. Our memberships in national networks such as International Relocation Services, Employee Relocation Council (ERC), Relocation Information Service (RIS) and National Referral Roster (NRR) offer effective member programs to serve corporate and relocation needs nationwide. The network also offers an incomparable combination of benefits to Burke Properties and other independent brokers.

Published by Burke Properties ™

Figure 4-1: *Page 1 of the completed My Newsletter.doc.*

What You Do	How You Do It
1. In Newsletter Layout.doc, **insert continuous section breaks after the Volume table and the heading/ subheading block.**	a. **Open** Newsletter Layout.doc.
	b. **Position your insertion point before the first return symbol after the Volume table.**
	c. **Choose Insert→Break.**
	d. Under Section Break Types, **select Continuous.**
	e. **Click OK.**
	f. **Repeat steps a through d to add a continuous section break after the heading/ subheading block.**
2. **View the section break marks on screen.**	a. **Click on Normal View button.** 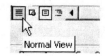

3. **What changes occur as a result of Normal view?**

4. **What does the status bar indicate regarding sections?**

5. Change the heading/subheading section's margins so that the entire heading appears on one line and return to Print Layout View.

a. Position your insertion point within the heading/subheading section.

b. Choose File→Page Setup.

c. On the Margins tab, **change the Left and Right margins to 1".**

d. Verify that the Apply To drop-down list is set to This Section.

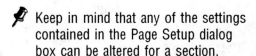 Keep in mind that any of the settings contained in the Page Setup dialog box can be altered for a section.

e. **Click OK.**

f. **Click the Print Layout View button.**

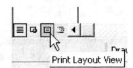

g. **Save the file as My Newsletter Layout.doc.**

6. **Have the margins changed for the other two sections?**

TOPIC B

Format Text into Newsletter Columns

Newsletter text appears in columns that normally will flow continuously from the bottom of one column to the top of the next column. In this topic you will convert existing text into newsletter columns.

When you are creating company newsletters, it is likely that you will be given electronic files created by others for submission into the newsletter. Therefore, it is important for you to know how to convert these existing files into newsletter columns of data.

Columns

Definition: *Newsletter columns* are a layout tool for controlling text flow within a document. They add design flexibility and visual interest to your pages while simultaneously increasing your text's readability; applying newsletter columns shortens line length making the text easier to read. Use newsletter columns for any project that may require more than one column, such as brochures, reports, and, of course, newsletters.

The contents of newsletter columns, (text, for example), will fill a column until it meets the column's lower boundary. When that happens, the contents will then automatically continue to flow into the top of the next column. If all columns on a page are filled, the remaining contents will begin to fill the first column of the next page.

> Columns are not displayed in Normal view. If you can't see the boundaries of the newsletter columns, make sure that the document is displayed in Print Layout view.

Example: Examples include newspaper or magazine articles, and company newsletters.

Format Text into Newsletter Columns

Creating Newsletter Columns using the Columns Button

To format text into newsletter columns, you can use one of two methods. The first method for creating newsletter columns is to use the Columns button which formats the text into newsletter columns, and also automatically attempts to create *balanced columns*—columns that have roughly equal amounts of text in each column. To do this:

1. Select the text you want formatted with newsletter columns.

2. Click the Columns button ▤ on the Standard toolbar and drag to select the desired number of columns.

Creating Newsletter Columns using the Menu

The second method for creating newsletter columns, the one that you will use in the next task, is to use the menu. This method is best for when there's just too much text to select easily. Even though it doesn't provide you with automatically balanced columns, it does give you immediate access to the other commands in the Columns dialog box, such as adjusting the spacing between columns, changing column width, and whether or not to put a line between columns. To use this method:

1. Place the insertion point in the page or section that you want to affect.

2. Choose Format→Columns to display the Columns dialog box and select the number of columns you want from the Presets area.

3. Click OK.

Line Breaks

There may be times when you want to start a new line before word wrap automatically starts a new line and without starting a new paragraph—such as when creating lists within a paragraph that has a hanging indent. The way to do that is to insert a line break. Inserting a *line break character* forces a new line break manually without creating a new paragraph. To insert a line break character, press [Shift]+[Enter].

ACTIVITY 4-2

Formatting Text into Newsletter Columns

Setup: My Newsletter Layout.doc is open in Print Layout View.

Scenario: Rather than type in lots of information, you copy the content of Newsletter Text.doc to My Newsletter Layout.doc. You then format the body text into a 2–column newsletter with a vertical line between columns. After reviewing the newsletter, you discover that the "Locations to Serve You" table is missing an office, so you add LosAngeles to the table data. You then save the file.

What You Do	How You Do It
1. Copy the entire contents of Newsletter Text.doc **into** My Newsletter Layout.doc **just below the heading block.**	a. **Open** Newsletter Text.doc.
	b. **Use whatever techniques you prefer to select and copy the entire document to the clipboard.**
	c. **Return to** My Newsletter Layout.doc.
	d. **Paste the data below the second return symbol below the heading/subheading section.**

2. Convert the copied text into a 2-column newsletter with a vertical line between the two columns.

   a. Select all of the body text.

     💣 Don't select the tables or heading/ subheading sections at the top of the document.

   b. Choose Format→Columns.

     📌 You can also click on the Columns button ▦ located on the Standard toolbar to create newsletter columns, however, you will not have as many options available as you will if you choose Format→Columns.

   c. In the Columns dialog box, under Presets, select Two.

   d. Check Line Between.

   e. Click OK.

3. Did you get the results you expected?

4. Edit the "Locations to Serve You" table to include the city of Los Angeles to the California row.

   a. In the Locations to Serve You table, in the California row, position your insertion point before "Palm Springs."

   b. Type *LosAngeles*.

   c. Press [Shift]+[Enter].

   d. Close Newsletter Text.doc.

   e. Save My Newsletter Layout.doc.

TOPIC C

Control Column Text Flow

Once you have applied newsletter-style columns you may find that this method doesn't always create balanced columns. Because you will need to control where columns break, in this topic you will insert column breaks to ensure that the column data appears uniform.

When you use newsletter columns, your columns may not always look balanced. Word offers various formatting options for ensuring that the text within your newsletter columns flows in a uniform manner. Inserting column breaks is one technique for ensuring balanced newsletter columns.

Column Breaks

As you've seen, applying newsletter columns can sometimes create unbalanced columns—more text in one column than in an adjacent column. You can balance columns yourself by inserting a *column break*. A column break is a manual break that you can insert to determine where one column will end and where the next column will begin.

Controlling Text Flow with Paragraph Formatting

Some more subtle ways to control text flow can be achieved at the paragraph level by adjusting line and page break options in the Paragraph dialog box. All of the line and page break options shown in Table 4-2 below are designed to keep text together. This is useful, for instance, if you don't want an automatic page break to interrupt an important point or idea that might be conveyed in a paragraph or series of paragraphs. By using one or several of these options, you can keep the idea from being split by a page break.

Table 4-2: *Paragraph Settings for Controlling Text Flow.*

Line and /Page Break Option	Effect When Selected
Window/Orphan Control	Won't allow Word to place the last line of a paragraph at the top of the next page by itself (known as a widow), or the first line of a paragraph at the bottom of a page by itself (known as an orphan).
Keep Lines Together	Won't allow an automatic page break to split a single paragraph over two pages.
Keep Text Together	Prevents an automatic page break from coming between the selected paragraph and the paragraph that immediately follows.
Page Break Before	Automatically inserts a manual page break before the selected paragraph.

The line and page break options in Table 4-2 can be applied as needed or they can be included as part of a style. However, since these paragraph settings would affect your entire document if they were included in a style, we recommend that you use them sparingly until you've practiced applying them, so that you are able to get the result you want.

Control Column Text Flow

Procedure Reference

To insert a column break:

1. If necessary, switch to print layout view.

2. Position your insertion point where you want to start the new column.

3. Choose Insert→Break.

4. Click Column Break.

5. Click OK.

ACTIVITY 4-3

Controlling Column Text Flow

Setup: My Newsletter Layout.doc is open.

Scenario: As you scroll through the newsletter, you find an area where the column breaks in a peculiar spot. You want the topic "Here's What a Realtor Does for You" to be grouped together in one column. To fix this, you insert a column break. You then preview the newsletter only to find that the page two columns aren't well balanced. To fix this, you insert another column break to balance the columns "The Regional." Finally, you save the file.

What You Do	How You Do It
1. Insert a column break before the topic "Here's What a Realtor Does for You" and before the table at the end of the document.	a. Position your insertion point before the topic "Here's What a Realtor Does for You."
	b. Choose Insert→Break.
	c. Under Break Types, **select Column Break.**
	d. **Click OK.**
	e. Follow steps a-d to insert a column break before the table at the end of the document.

2. **Preview the newsletter** to check column balance, and **balance the second column on page 2.**

a. On the Standard toolbar, **click on the Print Preview button** .

b. On the Print Preview toolbar, **click on the Multiple Pages button** and then **drag to select all six icons.** Column 2 of page 2 is too long.

c. **Close the Preview window.**

d. **Position your insertion point before the last paragraph of the "Buying a Home" topic.**

e. **Insert a column break.**

f. **Review the changes by previewing the newsletter.**

g. **Close the Preview window.**

h. **Save the file.**

TOPIC D

Wrap Text Around a Graphic

Previously in this course you inserted several types of graphics. Since Word offers various choices for wrapping text around graphics, in this topic you will wrap text around a graphic in a newsletter.

When you use graphics in documents, it is often necessary to have explanatory text or caption information near the graphic. Knowing how to use Word's various choices for wrapping text around graphics is will make the job of positioning text near graphics easier.

Wrap Text Around a Graphic

Procedure Reference
When you have explanatory text that goes along with a graphic, you may want to alter the way that the text flows in relation to that graphic. To "wrap" text around a graphic:

1. Select the picture or object.

   🖋 If the picture or object is on a drawing canvas, select the canvas.

2. Choose Format, and from the Format menu choose the command for the type of object you selected—for example Picture.

3. If necessary, select the Layout tab.

4. Click the wrapping tool that you want to apply.

5. Click OK.

ACTIVITY 4-4

Wrapping Text Around a Graphic

Setup: My Newsletter Layout.doc is open.

Scenario: To enhance your newsletter, My Newsletter Layout.doc, you insert a picture of the home office, Home Office.jpg, in the "Locations to Serve You" table. After inserting the picture, you wrap text around it. You then preview and save the file, returning to Print Layout view.

Locations to Serve You

California	Los Angeles Palm Springs San Diego San Francisco
Florida	Daytona Orlando
Kentucky	Lexington
Louisiana	New Orleans
Maryland	Baltimore Columbia
Massachusetts	 Boston Our home office in Boston's beautiful harbor district!
Ohio	Cleveland Toledo
Texas	Dallas San Antonio

Figure 4-2: *The Newsletter table, with a photo inserted.*

What You Do	How You Do It
1. Using Figure 4-2 as a guide, **insert the picture** Home Office.jpg in the newsletter table.	a. **Position your insertion point in the "Locations to Serve You" table, before the text "Boston—Our Home Office..."**
	b. **Choose Insert→Picture→From File.**
	c. **In the My Documents folder, insert Home Office.jpg.**
2. **How does the text around the image look?**	
3. **Format the picture so that the text is wrapped around the image.** **Preview the file.**	a. **Select the graphic.**
	b. **Choose Format→Picture.**
	c. **Select the Layout tab.**
	d. **Under Wrapping Style, select Square.**
	e. **Click OK.**
	f. **Save and preview the file.**

TOPIC E
Create Envelopes and Labels

You already know how to print documents from Word; but you may not know how to print envelopes or mailing labels. Frequently considered one of Word's more imposing features, creating envelopes and labels is like anything else—it just takes a little practice. Word offers a couple of convenient tools for printing envelopes and labels. In this topic, you will create envelopes and labels in Word.

It is more likely that when mailing a newsletter you will use the Mail Merge Wizard to print out mailing labels for each newsletter on your mailing list. (Mail Merge will be covered later in this course.) There will be times when you want to mail just one or two documents, therefore, you will need to know how to use Word to create envelopes and labels, when preparing just a few mailing pieces.

Mailing Labels

A mailing label is a sticky label that contains a mailing address used in place of an address on a mailed document. Word offers you several options for creating them. You can create single labels using the Tools→Letters and Mailings→Envelopes and Labels command. Or you can create multiple labels using the Mail Merge Wizard.

Create Envelopes and Labels

Creating Envelopes

When preparing only a few mailing pieces, choose the Tools, Envelopes And Labels command. This tool gives you the quickest way to create just a small number of envelopes or labels, for example, if you wanted to print one envelope for a letter or if you wanted to print a label to place on a disk mailer. However, the Envelopes And Labels tool isn't the best way to generate dozens or hundreds of pieces for a mass mailing because you have to build each envelope or label yourself, which can become quite time-consuming. To do a large mailing, Word's Tools→Mail Merge command is the most efficient method because you can let Word produce each mailing piece automatically based on an address list that you supply. The Mail Merge command is covered later in this course.

For professional looking envelopes, you don't need to buy them from a specialty printer or a stationery store. Word, combined with your computer's printer, can produce expert results. To create an envelope:

1. Choose Tools→Envelopes And Labels.

2. If necessary, select the Envelopes tab.

3. Fill in the Delivery and Return Address text boxes with the proper information.

 If your computer's address book is configured correctly, you can click on the address book icons to select delivery or return addresses.

4. Click Options to set the envelope size, fonts to be used for the addresses, and printing options, such as Envelope Manual Feed.

5. Click Print or Add To Document.

Creating Labels

Besides typical mailing labels, you can create labels for diskettes, post cards, audio or video tapes, name badges, tent cards, and so on. The variety of label types you can create is limited only by the label products you choose to use. To create a label for a disk mailer or for a small mailing

1. Choose Tools→Envelopes And Labels.

2. If necessary, select the Labels tab.

3. Fill in the Address text box.

4. Change the appropriate options to set the printer information, select label products (Word supplies templates for several companies mailing labels—Avery Standard is the default), and set label size.

5. Click New Document or Print.

ACTIVITY 4-5

Creating Envelopes and Labels

Setup: My Newsletter Layout.doc.

Scenario: Although you realize that you will be using the mail merge feature to create labels for the distribution of this newsletter, you investigate the options for creating individual envelopes and labels. When you are finished, you save the My Newsletter Layout.doc and close all other files without saving changes.

What You Do	How You Do It
1. Display the Envelopes tab of the Envelopes and Labels dialog box and use Figure 4-3. to enter both the delivery and return address data.	a. Choose Tools→Letters and Mailings→ Envelopes and Labels.
	b. If necessary, **select the Envelopes Tab.**
	c. If necessary, **select any text in the Delivery Address text box, replacing it with the delivery address shown in** Figure 4-3.
	d. Use Figure 4-3. to **enter the return address.**

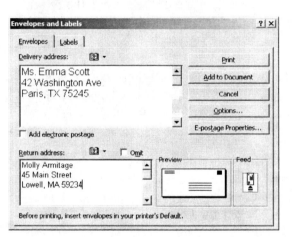

The Options button offers various envelope and printing options, and depending on the type of envelope and printer you use, you may need to set specific options.

Figure 4-3: *The Envelopes tab of the Envelopes and Labels dialog box.*

2. **Add the envelope to the document.**

a. **Click Add To Document**

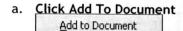

📌 Use the Print button if you need to print an envelope just once. Use the Add To Document button if you plan to reuse the envelope and document together. Add To Document inserts the envelope (and addresses) at the beginning of the active document so it can be printed and saved along with the active document.

b. If necessary, **answer No** to the "Do You Want To Save The New Return Address As The Default Return Address" dialog box.

c. **Observe the envelope.** The envelope is at the top of the document and the return address is separated from the document by a section break.

📌 To print an envelope, choose File→ Print and select the applicable options in the Print dialog box.

d. **Save the file.**

3. **Display and observe the Labels tab of the Envelopes and Labels dialog box.** It should look like Figure 4-4 below.

a. In the Envelopes and Labels dialog box, **select the Labels tab.** Because the envelope dialog box has data in the Address field, it is completed automatically in the Label Address field.

📌 The Options button offers various label options, and depending on the type of labels you use, you may need to set specific options.

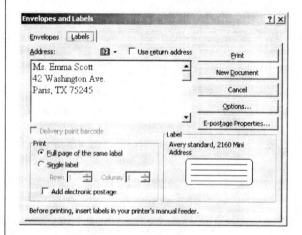

Figure 4-4: *The Labels tab of the Envelopes and Labels dialog box.*

4. **Create a new document called Labelsx.**

🖈 The x represents a number. The number will depend on how many new documents you have created.

a. **Click New Document**

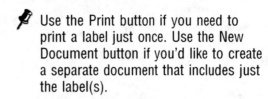

🖈 Use the Print button if you need to print a label just once. Use the New Document button if you'd like to create a separate document that includes just the label(s).

b. **Observe the document.** Because Full Page Of The Same Label was selected in the Envelopes And Labels dialog box, the inside address is repeated on each label.

🖈 To print a label, click Print on the Labels tab of the Envelopes and Labels dialog box, or from the Labelsx document, choose File→Print.

c. **Close** Labelsx.doc **without saving changes.**

d. **Save and close the file.**

Lesson 4 Follow-up

Using the skills that you obtained in this lesson, you can create a newsletter complete with columns and graphics.

1. **Why are sections beneficial?**

2. **List some printed materials you've seen that use newsletter columns.**

NOTES

LESSON 5
Sending Form Letters

Data Files:
Merge Letter.doc
Mailing List.xls
Outlook Contacts Folder

Lesson Time:
50–60 minutes

Lesson Objectives:

In this lesson, you will use the Mail Merge Wizard to mail merge form letters, complete with mailing labels.

You will:

- launch the Mail Merge Wizard and select the main document type.
- use the Mail Merge task pane to select the data source.
- use the Mail Merge task pane to insert the merge fields.
- use the Mail Merge task pane to merge the form letters and preview them.
- create mailing labels for your merged letters.

LESSON 5

Introduction

Let's take our attention off of templates, tables, graphics, and newsletters and focus it on sending form letters. All of us at one time or another have received a form letter of sorts, and there may be an instance when you will need to send out the same information to multiple people on your mailing list. You may need to send out a letter informing all of your existing clients of a recent company change or announcement. In this lesson you will be introduced to the process involved in sending form letters. You will then use a Word Wizard to perform the process.

Your manager asks that you send a personalized letter to all existing clients informing them of the new company Web site. With hundreds of clients on your mailing list it would take days to create individual letters for each client. Rather than type one letter for each client, you can save lots of time and energy using Word's mail merge feature.

TOPIC A

Select the Main Document Type

If you have information to send to one individual, you create a letter. However, if you have the same information to distribute to multiple recipients, you'll want to use a form letter. There are a series of steps involved in sending form letters. Thankfully, Word offers a Wizard to take you step-by-step through this process. So, the first step in sending form letters is to launch a wizard, at which point you will be asked to select the type of document you will create. In this topic you will launch the wizard and select the document type for your mailing.

The process for sending form letters, also referred to as performing a mail merge, includes many steps. Rather than trying to remember them all, you can use Word's Mail Merge Wizard to walk you through each step of the process eliminating the worry of forgetting an important step.

What is a Mail Merge?

A *mail merge*, named because they are primarily used to make pieces of mail, can be used to personalize form letters and similar documents, as well as to simplify large or repetitive tasks, such as producing catalogs, envelopes, and mailing labels.

A mail merge document is made up of two parts—a main document and a data source. Although we'll look at each of these components in greater detail soon, for now, all you need to know is that by combining the two, as shown in Figure 5-1, the result is a merged output document. To summarize, by creating a form letter (the main document) and connecting that main document to a list of recipients (the data source), you can create a completed merged document.

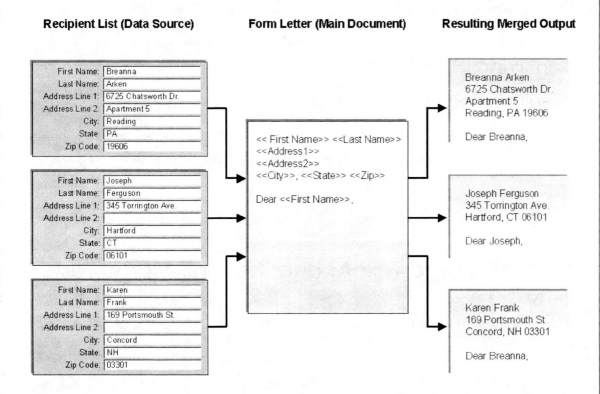

Recipient List (Data Source) — **Form Letter (Main Document)** — **Resulting Merged Output**

First Name: Breanna
Last Name: Arken
Address Line 1: 6725 Chatsworth Dr.
Address Line 2: Apartment 5
City: Reading
State: PA
Zip Code: 19606

First Name: Joseph
Last Name: Ferguson
Address Line 1: 345 Torrington Ave.
Address Line 2:
City: Hartford
State: CT
Zip Code: 06101

First Name: Karen
Last Name: Frank
Address Line 1: 169 Portsmouth St.
Address Line 2:
City: Concord
State: NH
Zip Code: 03301

<< First Name>> <<Last Name>>
<<Address1>>
<<Address2>>
<<City>>, <<State>> <<Zip>>

Dear <<First Name>>,

Breanna Arken
6725 Chatsworth Dr.
Apartment 5
Reading, PA 19606

Dear Breanna,

Joseph Ferguson
345 Torrington Ave.
Hartford, CT 06101

Dear Joseph,

Karen Frank
169 Portsmouth St.
Concord, NH 03301

Dear Breanna,

Figure 5-1: *How mail merge works.*

Example: Junk mail is a good example of when mail merge is used. The next time you get a piece of junk mail, see if your name is sprinkled throughout the piece. If your name's all over it, you can bet that a mail merge was used to "personalize" the letter.

The Main Document

To perform a mail merge, you need to have a main document.

Definition: This is where it all begins for a mail merge. The *main document* is the document that contains the content, text and graphics, that doesn't change from recipient to recipient. For example, the main document would contain the main body of a letter and a letter closing. Ultimately, the main document will also include the merge fields, which will be discussed soon. For now, think of a merge field as a placeholder that instructs Microsoft Word on where to put data source information within the main document, like names or mailing addresses, when the merge takes place. Merge fields generally are not inserted until after the data source has been created or identified.

Main Document Types Form Letters, some E-mail messages, Envelopes, Mailing Labels, or Directories.

Non-Example: A hand-written letter from a friend.

Faxes Microsoft Word's Mail Merge Wizard also supports group fax distribution, though the Faxes option isn't available in the Mail Merge Wizard unless faxing support is installed. See the on-line Help topic titled "Create and Distribute Merged Faxes" for help on this topic.

DISCOVERY ACTIVITY 5-1

Identifying Main Documents

Scenario: You decide that you need some practice identifying main documents.

1.   **List some examples of main documents that you encounter in your life.**

The Mail Merge Wizard and the Mail Merge Task Pane

Microsoft Word provides you with a tool for performing the mail merge process—the Mail Merge Wizard. Using the Wizard is the quickest way to perform a mail merge, however, is not the only way. The Mail Merge toolbar can also can be used to perform a mail merge.

When accessed, the Mail Merge Wizard is displayed in a task pane called the Mail Merge task pane, which walks you through the six steps of the mail merge process. Figure 5-2 displays step one in the mail merge process.

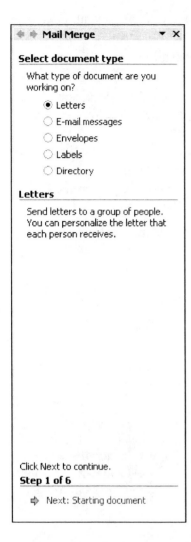

Figure 5-2: *The Step 1 Mail Merge task pane.*

The Mail Merge toolbar
If you are familiar with the mail merge process or prefer to work outside of the wizard, you can use the Mail Merge toolbar. The buttons are arranged in sequence from left to right. Use screen tips to identify each button.

Select the Main Document Type

Procedure Reference
The fastest way to perform a mail merge is to use the Mail Merge Wizard. After launching the Wizard, you will need to use the Mail Merge task pane to specify the main document type. To launch the Mail Merge Wizard and identify the main document type:

1. If you wish to use an existing document for your mail merge main document, open it now. Otherwise, open a blank document. (This procedure lists the steps for beginning with a blank document.)

2. Choose Tools→Letters and Mailings→Mail Merge Wizard to display the Step 1 Mail Merge task pane.

3. Choose one of the five options to specify the type of output documents that you wish to create.

4. Click on Next: Starting Document.

5. In the Step 2 Mail Merge task pane, select one of the following options to tell the wizard how to create your mail merge main document:

    - Select Use The Current Document to convert the active document to a mail merge main document.

    - Select Start From A Template to create a new main document based on a template. You would then need to use the Select Template command to select the template.

    - Select Start From Existing Document to create a new main document based on an existing document file and then select the document from the list that appears. If a document doesn't appear in the list, select the More Files option. Then click the Open button.

6. Click on Next: Select Recipients to prepare for the next step in the process.

ACTIVITY 5-2

Selecting the Main Document Type

Setup: Word is running, but there are no files open.

Scenario: You are asked by your manager to send a form letter announcing your new company web site to all existing clients. You've already created and saved the form letter body text, naming it Merge Letter.doc. So, you launch the Mail Merge Wizard where you are prompted to select the main document type, and once your screen matches Figure 5-2, you proceed to the Step 2 Mail Merge task pane.

What You Do	How You Do It
1. Create a new blank document and then launch the Mail Merge Wizard.	a. Click on the New Blank Document button. b. Choose Tools→Letters and Mailings→ Mail Merge Wizard.
2. What appears in the task pane area of your screen?	
3. Based on the scenario above, what type of document do we want to work on?	

4. **Accept the default document type of Letter and proceed to the Step 2 Mail Merge task pane.**

a. Under Select Document Type, **verify that Letters is selected.**

   📌 Your screen should match Figure 5-2.

b. Located near the bottom of the task pane, **click Next: Starting Document.**

5. **Select the existing document, Merge Letter.doc, as the starting document and then proceed to the Step 3 Mail Merge task pane.**

a. Under Select Starting Document, **select Start From Existing Document.**

b. Under Start From Existing, **click Open and open** Merge Letter.doc. The contents of the Merge Letter.doc are displayed in the document window.

   📌 To use a document that doesn't appear in the Open list, select the More Files option.

c. Located near the bottom of the task pane, **click Next: Select Recipients** to proceed to the Step 3 Mail Merge task pane.

   📌 To modify a selection in the Mail Merge task pane, click the Previous command near the bottom of the task pane. Using this command will display the previous step task pane.

TOPIC B

Select the Data Source

Now that you have selected the main document, the next step in the mail merge process is to specify who the form letters will be sent to. In this topic you will use the Mail Merge task pane to specify who will receive the form letters. You will also manipulate and modify the recipient data from within the Mail Merge task pane.

Specifying who your form letter will go to is a critical step in the mail merge process. Your mailing lists might reside in an Excel workbook, or in an Outlook Contacts folder, or you may need to create it from scratch. No problem, because Microsoft Word can handle it.

Aside from specifying the recipients of your form letters, you may want to send form letters only to those recipients who live within a certain state or zip code. Or maybe you want to sort the recipient list by a particular field, like last name. You can accomplish these needs by either filtering or sorting your recipient data.

The Data Source

To perform a mail merge, you need to have a data source.

Definition: The data source, also called the recipient list, is a critical piece of the mail merge process. Without it, you couldn't perform the mail merge. It is the file that contains the information to be merged into the output document and can contain information like names, addresses, and dates. You can think of a data source as a table of information. Each column of data in the data source corresponds to a category of information, like first name, last name, or street address for example. These can be referred to as fields. When you complete the merge, individual recipient information is mapped to the merge fields you include in your main document.

Example: A Microsoft Access database file, a Microsoft Excel workbook, or a Microsoft Outlook Contact list.

DISCOVERY ACTIVITY 5-3

Identifying Data Sources

Scenario: You decide that you need some practice identifying data sources.

---

1.   **List some examples of data sources that you encounter in your life.**

Select the Data Source

Procedure Reference
The next step in performing a mail merge is to select the data source, or recipient list. The Step 3 Mail Merge task pane is where you begin. To specify the data source:

1.   Verify that Step 3 of the Mail Merge task pane is active.

2.   Under Select Recipients, choose one of the three options to specify the data source: (This procedure lists the steps for using an existing list.)

   •   Select Use An Existing List to use an existing file that contains data you want to merge. Then, click the Browse command and select the file.

   •   Choose Select From Outlook Contacts to use a Microsoft Outlook Contacts folder as the source of the mail merge. Then, select the Choose Contacts Folder command to pick the folder that you want.

   •   Select Type a New List to create a new list by typing in the data. Then, select the Create command and type each entry into the New Address List dialog box. (The wizard will save the recipient list as an Access database file.)

3.   The wizard will then display the Mail Merge Recipients dialog box, where you can choose to sort or filter the data source information. When you've completed working with the data in the Mail Merge Recipients dialog box, click OK.

4.   Click on Next: Write Your Letter to prepare for the next step in the process.

Data Source Guidelines
If you create your own data sources, keep the following rules in mind to ensure data sources that give consistent and correct results:

   •   Use a unique name for each field.

   •   Begin field names with a letter.

   •   Use up to 40 characters in field names.

   •   Do not use spaces in field names.

   •   Avoid using blank records in the data source.

LESSON 5

Sorting the Data Source

If you've had any experience with data sources, (spreadsheets, for instance) then you know that they're not always organized in a way that you can find what you're looking for quickly. Fortunately, Word can help. The Mail Merge Recipient dialog box allows you to sort the data source records in various ways. Simply clicking on a column heading will arrange the records in alphabetical order for A-Z (ascending) and with a second click from Z-A (descending). If the column contains numbers, then the data is sorted chronologically. To perform a second or third sort, click on the drop-down arrow to the left of the field that you want to sort by, choose Advanced, and in the Filter and Sort dialog box, select the Sort Records tab. Use this tab to specify the sort field and sort order.

Filtering the Data Source

A mail merge need not include every record in a data source. In fact, you're more likely to use mail merges to include just the records which meet a particular criterion. You can do this by using the Mail Merge Recipient dialog box to apply a *filter*. To include only specific data records in a merge:

1. In the Mail Merge Recipient dialog box, click on the drop-down arrow to the left of any column heading.

2. Choose Advanced.

3. In the Filter and Sort dialog box, select the Filter Records tab.

4. Indicate a field name that is in the data source.

5. Choose a comparison phrase, such as Equal To.

6. Enter text for the comparison to be made.

7. Click OK.

> To clear a filter, click on the Clear All button on the Filter Records tab of the Filter and Sort dialog box, or click on the drop-down arrow to the left of any column heading and choose All.

> Be aware that to select the data source, you will choose to do either Activity 5–4, Select and Customize the Data Source, or Activity 5–5, Selecting Outlook Contacts as the Data Source.

ACTIVITY 5-4

Select and Customize the Data Source

Setup: You will choose to do either this activity or the next activity to select the data source. This activity uses an Excel worksheet as the data source, where the next activity uses an Outlook Contacts folder as the data source. Note that there is extra classroom setup involved should you choose to do the next activity. All activities that follow will work regardless of the activity you choose.

Setup: The Step 3 Mail Merge task pane is open, and the contents of the Merge Letter.doc are displayed in the document window.

Scenario: You're now ready to specify who the form letters will go to—your clients. You already have a client list that resides in an Excel worksheet named Mailing List.xls that includes client name and address information, as well as the date of the last telephone communication you had with each client. You will use the Step 3 Mail Merge task pane to specify this existing file as your data source.

Figure 5-3: *The Step 3 Mail Merge task pane.*

What You Do	How You Do It
1. Display the Select Data Source dialog box.	a. Under Select Recipients, **verify that Use An Existing List is selected.** b. Under Use An Existing List, **click on Browse.**
2. **From the My Documents folder, open sheet 1 of** Mailing List.xls.	a. In the Select Data Source dialog box, **navigate to the My Documents folder and open the** Mailing List.xls **file.** b. In the Select Table dialog box, **click on OK** to open Sheet 1 of the Mailing List.xls file. The Mail Merge Recipients dialog box is displayed.

3. **What is contained in the Mail Merge Recipients dialog box, shown in Figure 5-4?**

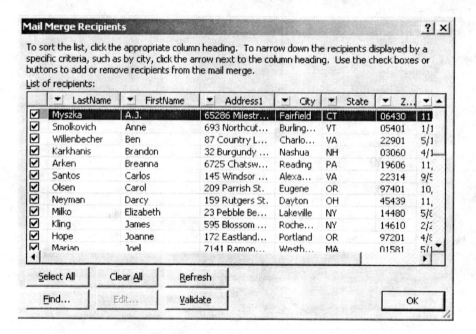

Figure 5-4: *The Mail Merge Recipients dialog box.*

4. **What order is the data in? (If necessary, use the scroll bars in the Mail Merge Recipients dialog box to view all of the data.)**

ACTIVITY 5-5

Selecting Outlook Contacts as the Data Source

Setup: You will choose to do either this activity or the previous activity to select the data source. This activity uses an Outlook Contacts folder as the data source, where the previous activity, uses an Excel worksheet as the data source. Note that there is extra classroom setup involved should you choose to do this activity. All activities that follow will work regardless of the activity you choose.

Setup: The setup instructions in the beginning of this course have been performed for accessing Microsoft Outlook data.

Setup: The Step 3 Mail Merge task pane is open, and the contents of the Merge Letter.doc are displayed in the document window.

Scenario: You're now ready to specify who the form letters will go to—your clients. Your client list resides in your Outlook Contacts folder. You will use the Step 3 Mail Merge task pane to specify this existing data as your data source.

What You Do	How You Do It
1. **Select the Outlook Contacts folder as the data source.**	a. Under Select Recipients, **choose "Select From Outlook Contacts."**
	b. **Click on Next:Write Your Letter.**
	c. **Wait for Outlook to retrieve data from the Microsoft Exchange Server.**
	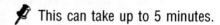 This can take up to 5 minutes.
	d. If necessary, in the Choose Profile dialog box, **select your user id and click OK.**
	e. If prompted for a password, **enter your password and click OK.**
	f. In the Select contact List Folder dialog box, **click OK to accept the contacts folder.**
	g. **Wait for Outlook to retrieve data from the Microsoft Exchange Server.**
	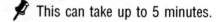 This can take up to 5 minutes.

2. **What is contained in the Mail Merge Recipients dialog box shown in Figure 5-5?**

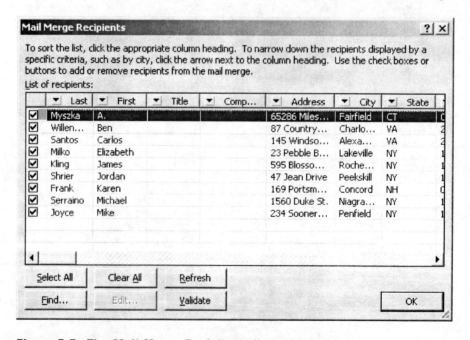

Figure 5-5: *The Mail Merge Recipients dialog box.*

---

3. **What order is the data in? (If necessary, use the scroll bars in the Mail Merge Recipients dialog box to view all of the data.)**

ACTIVITY 5-6

Sorting and Filtering a Data Source

Setup: The Step 3 Mail Merge task pane is open and the Mail Merge Recipients dialog is displayed and contains the Mailing List.xls data.

Scenario: You've heard that it is possible to sort and filter the data source data to either rearrange it or to include only those records that satisfy a specific criteria in the mail merge. You decide to sort the data source data in alphabetical order by last name. You then experiment with filtering the data to include clients who reside in New York State only. Since you need to get this letter out to all of your clients at the same time, you clear the filter.

What You Do | **How You Do It**

1. **Change the order of the data so that it is listed in alphabetical order by last name.**

   a. **Click on the Last Name column heading to sort the data alphabetically by last name.**

   ● Do not click on the down-pointing arrow to the left of the LastName heading as that will apply filtering. If you did press on it, just press [Esc].

2. Using Figure 5-6, **apply a filter to display only those clients who reside in New York State.**

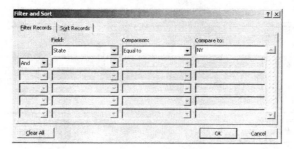

Figure 5-6: *The Filter and Sort dialog box.*

a. **Click on the down-pointing arrow to the left of the State column heading.**

b. **Choose (Advanced...).**

c. **Display the Field drop-down list and scroll to select State.**

d. **In the Compare to field, type *NY*.**

    🖈 Your screen should match Figure 5-6.

e. **Click on OK.** Five clients reside in New York State.

3. **Remove the filter so that all records appear in the Mail Merge dialog box.**

a. **Click on the down-pointing arrow to the left of the State column heading.**

b. **Choose (All).** The filter is removed.

4. **Accept the changes and proceed to the Step 4 Mail Merge task pane.**

a. **Click OK** to close the Mail Merge Recipients dialog box.

b. **Click on Next: Write Your Letter.**

TOPIC C

Insert Merge Fields

You've specified the main document and the data source for your mail merge. You now need to connect the two. In this topic you will insert information into the main document that will cause Word to retrieve information from the data source when the merge takes place.

Form letters normally include address and name information. The beauty of a using a mail merge to create form letters is that you don't have to type individual name and address information in each letter. Rather, you pull the information in from the data source. In order for the main document to have access to the information contained in the data source you need to include the necessary data source fields within the main document. This is referred to as inserting merged fields.

Merge Fields

To connect the main document with the data source, you must include merge fields in the main document.

Definition: In a Word mail merge, a merge field is a placeholder that instructs Microsoft Word to insert text, graphics, page numbers, and other material into the main document automatically. If you have a data field in the data source called Last Name, Word replaces every occurrence of the field <<Last Name>> in the form letter with the Last Name data in the current record of the data source.

Example: A data source field, an address block, or a greeting line.

Merge Field Commands Aside from the database fields that can be included as merge fields in the main document, Microsoft Word offers some time-saving commands that allow you to specify elements and formatting for the blocks you want to include in your mail merge. These fields include Address blocks, Greeting lines, Electronic postage, and Postal bar codes. Table 5-1.describes these commands and what they do.

Table 5-1: *The Commands in the Step 4 Mail Merge Task Pane.*

To Insert These Merge Fields	Click This Command in the Step 4 Task Pane
Name and address fields, in various formats.	Address Block
Salutation field, in various formats.	Greeting Line
E-postage field.	Electronic Postage
Postal bar code field.	Postal Bar Code
Merge fields for specific fields in your recipient list.	More Items

Insert Merge Fields

Procedure Reference To insert a merge field into the main document of a mail merge:

1. Verify that Step 4 of the Mail Merge task pane is active.

2. Position your insertion point where you want the first merge field to appear.

3. Under Write Your Letter, select the appropriate merge field command: (This procedure lists the steps for using the More Items choice.)

   • Select Address Block to insert formatted address-related fields.

   • Select Greeting Line to insert formatted salutation fields.

   • Select Electronic Postage to insert an electronic postage fields.

   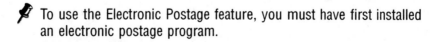 To use the Electronic Postage feature, you must have first installed an electronic postage program.

   • Select Postal Bar Code to insert a postal bar code at the insertion point of a data fields.

   • Select More Items to insert Database fields (those from your data source) or Address Fields (those that automatically map to corresponding fields in your data source, even if the data source's fields don't have the same name as your fields).

🔖 If the Match Fields dialog box appears when you are inserting merge fields, Microsoft Word may have been unable to find information that it needs for the merge field. Click the arrow next to (not available), and then select the field from your data source that corresponds to the field required for the mail merge.

4. Select the appropriate merge field from the Insert Merge Field dialog box, click Insert, click Close, and add any nonprinting symbols (spaces or returns).

5. Repeat steps 2 through 4 for any additional merge fields.

ACTIVITY 5-7

Inserting Merge Fields

Setup: The Step 4 Mail Merge task pane is open. The contents of Merge Letter.doc appear in the document window and Mailing List.xls has been set up as the data source.

Scenario: You now have the main document and the data source specified. But currently there is no link between the two. To link them, you need to enter the appropriate merge fields in the main document. Rather than insert the FirstName, LastName, Address1, City, State, and Zip fields separately for the address information, you use the Address Block to insert them into the main document.

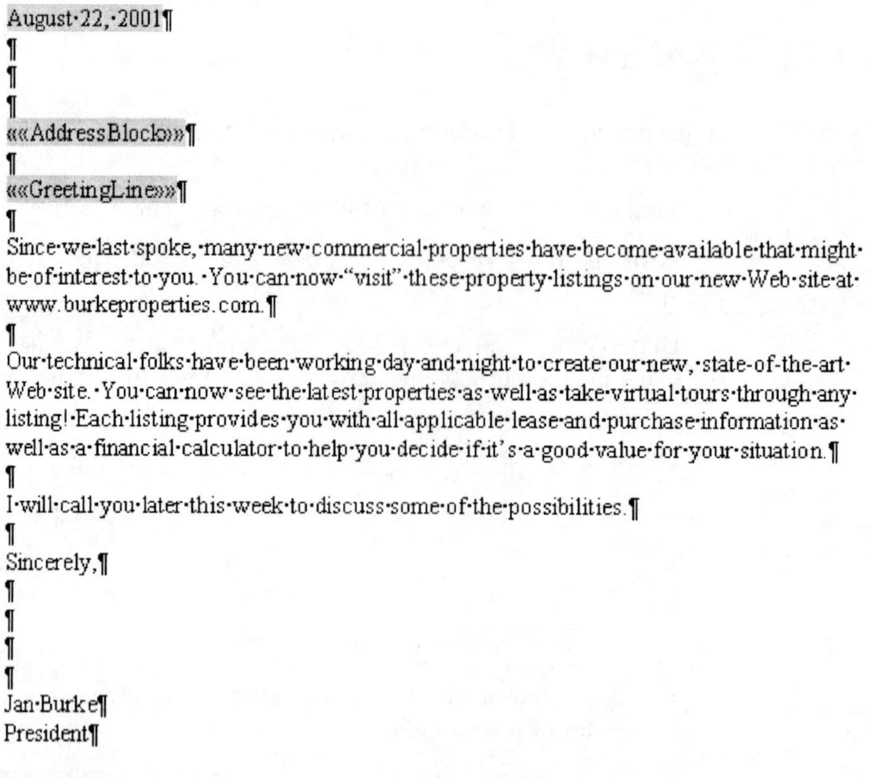

August·22,·2001¶
¶
¶
¶
««AddressBlock»»¶
¶
««GreetingLine»»¶
¶
Since·we·last·spoke,·many·new·commercial·properties·have·become·available·that·might·
be·of·interest·to·you.·You·can·now·"visit"·these·property·listings·on·our·new·Web·site·at·
www.burkeproperties.com.¶
¶
Our·technical·folks·have·been·working·day·and·night·to·create·our·new,·state-of-the-art·
Web·site.·You·can·now·see·the·latest·properties·as·well·as·take·virtual·tours·through·any·
listing!·Each·listing·provides·you·with·all·applicable·lease·and·purchase·information·as·
well·as·a·financial·calculator·to·help·you·decide·if·it's·a·good·value·for·your·situation.¶
¶
I·will·call·you·later·this·week·to·discuss·some·of·the·possibilities.¶
¶
Sincerely,¶
¶
¶
¶
¶
Jan·Burke¶
President¶

Figure 5-7: *The main document with inserted merge fields.*

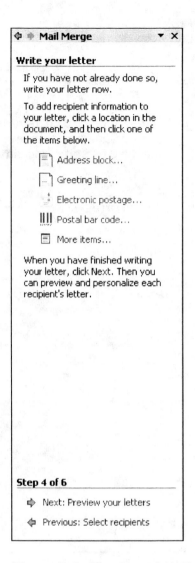

Figure 5-8: *The Step 4 Mail Merge task pane.*

What You Do	How You Do It
1. **Enter today's date with a date format of your choice.** **Add five blank lines after the date.**	a. **Choose Insert→Date and Time.** b. **Under Available Formats, select the third date format from the top and click OK.** c. **Press [Enter] five times.**

2. You are now ready to insert the address block merge field. **Verify that your insertion point is before the Return symbol immediately preceding the first sentence of the letter.**

   Display and observe the Insert Address Block dialog box and then accept the default settings.

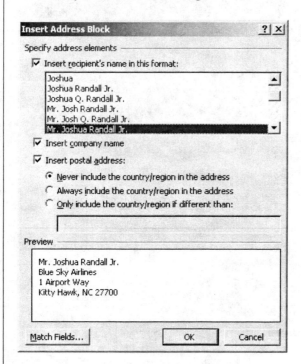

a. **Position your insertion point accordingly.**

b. Under Write Your Letter, **click on Address Block.** The Insert Address Block dialog box is displayed. By default, the address block field includes the client name, client company (if applicable), the first address line, and the city, state, and zip code.

c. **Click on OK.** The Address Block field has been inserted into the main document.

---

3. **Insert the default Greeting line, using** Figure 5-7 **as a placement guide.**

a. **Press [Enter] twice to add space between the address block and the salutation.**

b. Under Write Your Letter, **select Greeting Line.**

c. **Click OK.** The Greeting Line field has been inserted into the main document.

d. **Press [Enter] once to add space between the salutation and the body of the letter.**

TOPIC D

Merge and Preview Form Letters

You've completed the setup involved in a mail merge and are now ready to perform the actual merging of the main document and data source information. In this topic you will merge and then preview your form letters in order to verify accuracy prior to printing.

What if you printed 500 form letters only to find that you had inserted the address merge fields in the wrong location? Well, this is why it is important to preview your merged documents prior to printing. If you find any errors, you can fix them before wasting time and paper!

Merge and Preview Form Letters

Procedure Reference

When the wizard displays the Step 5 Mail Merge task pane, it replaces each of the merge fields in the main document with the actual text from the first entry of the data source, so you can see what your first output document will look like. To preview you form letters:

1. Verify that Step 5 of the Mail Merge task pane is active.

2. Click the right-pointing arrow button to view the next letter or the left-pointing arrow to view the previous letter.

3. To find an entry in your data source that contains specific text and to view the output document showing that entry's information, click the Find A Recipient command and type the text into the Find Entry dialog box.

4. To modify the recipient list, click the Edit Recipient List command.

   📌 When you edit the recipient list, you affect the output data, not the original data in the data source. To edit the data source data, open the application that contains that data.

5. To remove the currently displayed output document from the final output, click the Exclude This Recipient button.

6. When you are finished previewing the output documents, click the Next command to display the final Mail Merge Task pane where you can click on Print to print your letters.

ACTIVITY 5-8

Merging and Previewing Form Letters

Setup: The complete merge letter is displayed in the document window and the Step 4 Mail Merge task pane is displayed.

Scenario: You are now ready to perform the mail merge. You proceed to step 5 of the mail merge process and preview the merged letters in the document window prior to printing them. You realize that one of the letters is addressed to Karen Frank, who is no longer a client; so you edit that information directly from the Mail Merge task pane. Once you've made the edit, you complete the mail merge, save the file as My Mail Merge.doc, and then investigate the printing options. When finished, you close the file.

Figure 5-9: *The Step 5 Mail Merge task pane.*

What You Do	How You Do It

1. **Preview your letters by clicking on Next: Preview Your Letters.**

What has changed in the document window?

---

2. **Preview the next two letters.**

    a. On the Mail Merge task pane, under Preview Your Letters, **click the right-pointing arrow button** $\boxed{>>}$ to preview the second letter.

    b. **Click the right-pointing arrow button again** to preview the third letter.

---

3. Because this entry is no longer a client, **exclude this letter from the merge.**

    a. Under Make Changes, click **Exclude This Recipient** $\boxed{\text{Exclude this recipient}}$.

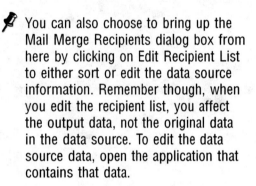 You can also choose to bring up the Mail Merge Recipients dialog box from here by clicking on Edit Recipient List to either sort or edit the data source information. Remember though, when you edit the recipient list, you affect the output data, not the original data in the data source. To edit the data source data, open the application that contains that data.

---

4. Display the Step 6 Mail Merge task pane and then Save the File as *My Mail Merge.doc*.

a. Click Next: Complete The Merge.

b. Save the file as *My Mail Merge.doc*.

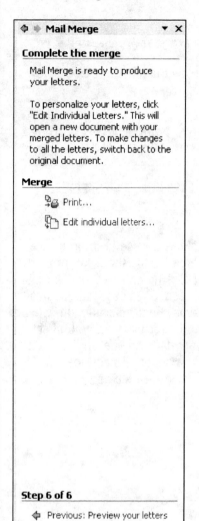

Figure 5-10: *The Step 6 Mail Merge task pane.*

5. **Display, observe, and close the Merge to Printer dialog box.**

    When finished, **close the My Mail Merge file.**

a. **Under Merge, click Print.**

Note that you can print all of the letters, print the current letter, or enter a range of letters to print.

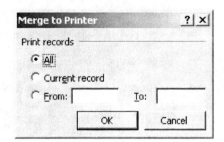

b. **Click Cancel.**

c. **Close the file.**

 To personalize your letters, you can click on Edit Individual Letters. This will open a new document with your merged letters. To make changes to all the letters, switch back to the main document and make edits in it directly.

TOPIC E

Create Mailing Labels

You've printed all of your letters and now need to mail them. Rather than print individual envelopes or labels, you can save time by using the Mail Merge Wizard to create them all at once using the same data source as you did for your form letter. In this topic you will create mailing labels using the Mail Merge Wizard.

Now that you've got your letters ready, how are you going to address all of those envelopes? Sure you could hire a calligrapher, but you're manager has asked that you keep the budget to a minimum. Rather than create individual mailing labels by re-entering all of those addresses, you can use the Mail Merge Wizard to create them all quickly. You already know much of this process, since it is very similar to the process for creating form letters.

Create Mailing Labels

Procedure Reference

Creating mailing labels is very similar to creating form letters—you use the Mail Merge Wizard.

1. Launch the Mail Merge Wizard and choose Labels as your document type.

2. Proceed to Step 2 of the task pane.

3. Under Change document layout, click on Label Options and use the Label Options dialog box to set the printer and label information.

4. Proceed to Step 3 of the task pane.

5. Select your data source.

6. Proceed to Step 4 of the task pane.

7. Under Arrange Your Labels, select the appropriate merge field command and insert the merge fields.

8. Click on the Update All Labels button to copy the layout of the first label to the other labels on the page.

9. Proceed to Step 5 of the task pane.

10. Preview and edit your labels.

11. Proceed to Step 6 of the task pane and print your labels.

ACTIVITY 5-9

Creating Mailing Labels

Setup: Word is running and no files are open.

Scenario: Now that you've printed out all of the letters, you need to mail them. So, you launch the Mail Merge Wizard and walk through the necessary steps involved in creating mailing labels. Since all of your address information resides in Mailing List.xls, you will identify that file as your data source. You will then add merge fields to create the labels. You save the file as My Mailing Lables.doc and close all other open files without saving changes.

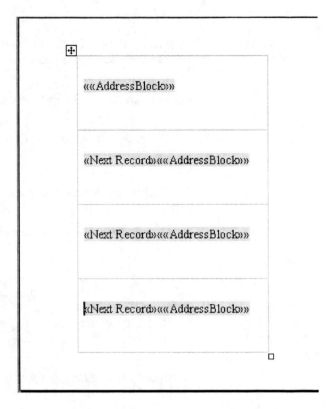

Figure 5-11: *A mailing label with inserted merge fields.*

Figure 5-12: *Completed mailing labels.*

What You Do	How You Do It
1. Launch the Mail Merge Wizard and proceed to the Step 2 Mail Merge task pane.	a. From the New Document task pane, under New, **click on Blank Document.**
	b. **Launch the Mail Merge Wizard.**
	c. Under Select Document Type, **select Labels.**
	d. **Click Next: Starting Document.**
2. Microsoft Word supports hundreds of label types. What type of labels do you currently use at work?	
3. Display the Label Options dialog box, accept the default label information, and proceed to the Step 3 Mail Merge task pane.	a. Under Select Starting Document, **verify that Change Document Layout is selected.**
	b. Under Change Document Layout, **click on Label options.**
	📄 Label options...
	c. **Click OK.**
	d. **Click Next: Select Recipients.**
4. Select Mailing List.xls as your data source, sorting the data in alphabetical order by last name.	a. **Verify that Use An Existing Document is selected and click on Browse.**
	b. **Open** Mailing List.xls.
	c. **Sort the data by the LastName column.** (Click on the column heading.)
	d. **Click OK.**
5. Populate the first label with the appropriate mailing address merge fields. See Figure 5-11 for reference.	a. **Click Next: Arrange Your Labels.**
	b. **Insert the Address Block.**
6. Copy the layout of the first label to all remaining labels on the page.	a. Under Replicate Labels, **click on Update All Labels.**

7. Proceed to the Step 5 Mail Merge task pane and preview the labels.

   a. Click Next: Preview Your Labels.

   b. Use the preview arrows to preview your labels.

8. Identify the print label options. Do not print the labels.

   a. Click Next: Complete The Merge.

   b. **Click Print.** Note that you can print all of the labels, print the current label, or enter a range of labels to print.

   c. **Click Cancel, save the file as My Mailing Lables.doc.**

9. How do your labels compare with Figure 5-12?

   Close the file.

Lesson 5 Follow-up

With the skills acquired in this lesson, you can perform a Mail Merge by identifying the main document, identifying and customizing the data source, and inserting merge fields.

1. Why is mail merge such a useful tool?

2. What components are necessary to make a merged document?

NOTES

LESSON 6
Creating a Web Page

Data Files:
Web Page Text.doc
Lesson Time:
20–30 minutes

Lesson Objectives:

In this lesson, you will create a Web page, create and edit a hyperlink, save and preview a Web page, as well as enhance a Web page by applying themes.

You will:

* create, save, and preview a Web page in Word.
* view your newly created Web page in a browser.
* insert a hyperlink into a Web page.
* edit an existing hyperlink in a Web Page.
* enhance a Web page by applying a theme.

Introduction

Using the Internet as a communications tool has become standard practice these days. Many organizations have Web sites that provide their product information so that clients can research and order directly from the site. In this lesson you will explore how Word can be used for posting information on the Internet.

In this day and age all of us at one time or another need to share information. You may have some company information that you want to share with the masses, or you may want to create a Web site for your organization for both existing and potential clients to access.

TOPIC A

Create a Web Page Using a Template

Although there are dedicated applications designed for creating Web pages, like Microsoft FrontPage, you can create Web pages using Word. You can create a Web page from scratch, or use a Word Web template. As it does with other documents, Word provides several templates for creating new Web pages. In this topic you will create a Web page for your organization using the Simple Layout template.

You don't need to be a programmer to create Web pages these days. As it does with other document types, Word provides several templates for creating new Web pages. Suppose that your manager wants you to create a basic Web page that gives general information about your organization to post on the Internet. Since you're not certain where to begin, you will use a Word template to help you get started.

Create a Web Page Using a Template

Creating a Web Page using a Word Template

You can create a Web page in one of several ways; using the Web Page Wizard, using a Web page template, using a new blank document, or using an existing Word document. In this topic, you will base the Web page on a Web template. To create a Web page using a Web template:

1. Choose File, New.

2. In the New Document task pane, under New From Template, click General Templates.

3. On the Web Pages tab, double-click the template that you want to base your Web page on.

   ✏ If you wish to use the Web Page Wizard to walk you through the steps of creating your Web page, double-click on Web Page Wizard.

4. Replace any filler text with your Web page information, adding whatever elements that you desire.

5. Choose File→ Save As Web Page and name and save the file.

Creating a Blank Web Page

To create a blank Web page:

1. Choose File, New.

2. Under New in the New Document task pane, click Blank Web Page.

Creating a Web Page from an Existing Document

To create a Web page from an existing document:

1. Open the document that you wish to base the Web page on.

2. Choose File→Save As Web Page and name and save the file.

Previewing Web Pages

Once you save a document as a Web page, or use a Word Web template to create a Web page, Word automatically switches from Print Layout view to Web Layout view. The Web Layout view attempts to simulate how your Web page will be displayed by a browser; displaying AutoShapes, backgrounds, and other common Web page elements and objects. To use Web Layout View:

1. Choose View→Web Layout; or

2. Click the Web Layout View button [icon] just above the status bar.

ACTIVITY 6-1

Creating a Web Page Using a Template

Setup: Word is running, but there are no files open.

Scenario: Your manager requests that you create a simple Web page for your organization. So you create one using Word 's Simple Layout Web template. You already have a document named Web Page Text.doc, that contains the information that you want to use for your Web page, so you copy it into the Simple Layout Web template and save it as My Simple Web Page.htm.

Lesson 6

1. **Display the available Web Page templates and create a new file using Simple Layout.**

   a. **Choose File→New.**

   b. **From the Templates dialog box, select the Web Pages tab.**

   c. **Open Simple Layout.**

   d. **Observe the Web page in Web Layout View.** It is set in a one-row by three-row table, with the second column containing filler text.

   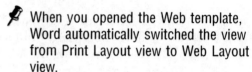 When you opened the Web template, Word automatically switched the view from Print Layout view to Web Layout view.

2. **Replace the filler text in column 2, with the contents of Web Page Text.doc.**

   a. **Delete the filler text in the second column.** (Press [Alt] and click anywhere in the column to select the column contents and then press Delete.)

   b. **Choose Insert→File.**

   c. **Double-click on** Web Page Text.doc.

3. **Save the file as a Web page named** My Simple Web Page.htm

   a. **Choose File→Save As Web Page.**

   b. **Observe the Save As Type box.** The document is already being saved as a Web page (*.htm; *.html).

   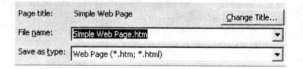

   c. **Name the file** My Simple Web Page.htm

   d. **Click Save.**

TOPIC B

Preview a Web Page in a Browser

Although the Web Layout view makes it convenient to look at a Web page as you work on it, we recommend that you preview your Web pages in a browser instead. Why? Because when Web pages are put on the Web, people who view them will be using a browser to do so—not Word's Web Layout view. Since previewing your work in a browser more accurately represents your visitors' experience when they view your pages, in this topic you will preview your newly created Web page in a browser.

While the vast majority of features are preserved when you save a document as a Web page (*.htm or *.html), there may be instances when a certain feature isn't supported by a browser. By viewing your work "through your visitor's eyes," you may discover discrepancies in the display and be able to fix them before you post the Web page. Therefore, it's important that you preview a newly created Web site prior posting it to the Web.

Preview a Web Page in a Browser

Procedure Reference

It's important that you preview a newly created Web site prior posting it to the Web. When you save a document as a Web page, there may be instances when a certain feature isn't supported by a browser. By viewing your work in the browser prior to posting it to the Web, you may discover discrepancies in the display and be able to fix them. To preview your Web page in the browser:

1. Choose File→Web Page Preview. Your default Web browser will be launched automatically and you will see how your Web page looks in the browser environment.

2. View the Web page in a Web browser.

3. When you're done previewing the Web page, close the browser to return to Word.

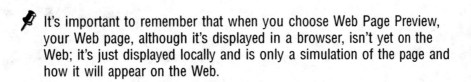 It's important to remember that when you choose Web Page Preview, your Web page, although it's displayed in a browser, isn't yet on the Web; it's just displayed locally and is only a simulation of the page and how it will appear on the Web.

ACTIVITY 6-2

Previewing a Web Page in a Browser

Setup: My Simple Web Page.htm is open.

Scenario: Since you want to get a realistic view of what visitors to the Web site will see, you preview My Simple Web Page.htm in the browser. And while in the browser you view the source code for the Web page.

What You Do	How You Do It
1. Preview your newly created Web page in the browser.	a. Choose File→Web Page Preview.
	b. If necessary, **maximize the browser window.**
2. Return to Word, and view the source code for the Web page. When finished, close the Microsoft Script Editor window.	a. On the Browser toolbar, **click on the Edit With Microsoft Word button** .
	b. **Choose View→HTML Source** to launch Microsoft Script Editor and the source code window.
	c. **Close the Microsoft Script Editor window.**
3. What is the purpose of the table at the bottom of the Web page?	

TOPIC C

Create a Hyperlink in a Web Page

You've got your Web page created, however, you would like to allow visitors to be able to easily reference other related information directly from your Web site. In this topic you will learn how to connect related data to a Web page.

As a real-estate agency, you know that your existing and potential clients are interested in housing and all that goes along with owning or renting a home. Because of this, you want to provide references to other related Web pages for them to access from within your Web page. By doing so, you'll assure return visits to your Web page.

Hyperlinks

When creating Web pages, you may find times when you want to reference other related information for the user to access. When this is true, you can create hyperlinks that, when clicked on, will display other related information for the user.

Definition: URLs, or *Uniform Resource Locators,* are used to identify the physical location of a resource that's connected to the Web. URLs are only useful if you can remember them, and since many of them can be quite long, that can be difficult to do. That's where *hyperlinks* come in—a hyperlink, referred to as a link, contains a Web resource's URL . By just clicking on the hyperlinked object, you can call that resource up in your browser. Hyperlinks are used to connect related information. Links can be other documents, spreadsheets, or files.

When viewing a Web page, hyperlinks are generally (though not always) underlined and displayed in a different color—blue, by default—than the other document text. Another way to identify a hyperlink is to watch your mouse pointer. When you place it over a hyperlink, the mouse pointer changes from an arrow to a pointing hand. To see a hyperlink's target URL displayed before you click on it, move the mouse pointer over the link and observe the browser's status message area, and in some cases, the ScreenTip.

Example: While reading a reference manual, you have a question on a word's definition. So, you look up the word in the glossary. The glossary provides you with a definition, but also refers you to another word, which you then look up in the glossary. In this example, using a hyperlink to the referenced word would allow you to click on the referenced word to go directly to the referenced words definition.

Create a Hyperlink in a Web Page

Procedure Reference Once you decide to create a hyperlink, it's very simple to do:

1. Select the text or picture you want to display as the hyperlink.

2. Open the Insert Hyperlink dialog box by:
   - clicking on the Insert Hyperlink button on the Standard toolbar;
   - choosing Insert→Hyperlink; or

- pressing [Ctrl]+K.

3. Type the URL of the hyperlink in the Address box.

🖈 You can also use the buttons under Look In to locate an address.

4. Click OK.

ACTIVITY 6-3

Creating a Hyperlink in a Web Page

Setup: My Simple Web Page.htm is open in the browser, and the browser window is maximized.

Scenario: Although you have made reference to three related resources within a table at the bottom of My Simple Web Page.htm, you haven't made the connection by creating hyperlinks. You create hyperlinks for the three references listed in the Some Other Web Sites to Visit table and return to Word, saving your file when finished.

What You Do	How You Do It
1. **Return to Microsoft Word and select the text "Microsoft HomeAdvisor."**	a. **Return to Microsoft Word.**
	b. Drag to **select the text "Microsoft HomeAdvisor."**
	💣 Be sure to drag to select. If you select the entire cell, the Insert Hyperlink command will be unavailable.
2. **In the Hyperlink dialog box, create a hyperlink using** *http:// homeadvisor.msn.com* **for the address.**	a. On the Standard toolbar, **Click on the Insert Hyperlink button** 🖳 .
	🖈 You can also press [Ctrl]+K to open the Insert Hyperlink dialog box.
	b. In the Address text box, **type** *http:// homeadvisor.msn.com.*
	c. **Click OK.**

3. **What indication do you get that the hyperlink has been inserted?**

4. Insert a hyperlink to Bob Vila's Home site: *http://www.bobvila. com* and one to the Home and Garden Television site: *http://www. hgtv.com.*

a. Drag to **select the text "Bob Villa's Home Site."**

b. **Display the Insert Hyperlink dialog box.**

c. In the address box, **type** *http://www. bobvila.com.*

d. **Follow steps a through c to create the hyperlink for Home & Garden Television using** *http://www.hgtv.com.*

e. **Save the file.**

TOPIC D

Edit a Hyperlink in a Web Page

Since the Web changes quickly and constantly, Web sites are often moved, added, or deleted. And as a result, you may have to edit an existing hyperlink. In this topic, you will learn to edit hyperlinks in a Web page.

You're Web page contains a hyperlink whose description isn't as clear as it could be. For example, you may have used "Home & Garden Television" as your hyperlinks displayed text, where it is better know by it's station abbreviation "HGTV." So, in order to keep your Web pages clear and accurate, you need to know how to edit hyperlinks.

Edit a Hyperlink in a Web Page

Procedure Reference

The Web changes quickly and constantly; Web sites are often moved, added, or deleted. To edit an existing hyperlink:

1. Position the mouse pointer over the hyperlink.

2. Right-click and choose Edit Hyperlink from the shortcut menu.

3. Make the necessary edits to the URL.

4. Click OK.

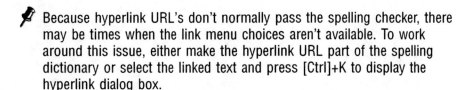 Because hyperlink URL's don't normally pass the spelling checker, there may be times when the link menu choices aren't available. To work around this issue, either make the hyperlink URL part of the spelling dictionary or select the linked text and press [Ctrl]+K to display the hyperlink dialog box.

ACTIVITY 6-4

Editing a Hyperlink in a Web Page

Setup: My Simple Web Page.htm is open in Word.

Scenario: In My Simple Web Page.htm, the table, Some Other Web Sites to Visit," refers to "Home & Garden Television" as that hyperlinks displayed text. Since it is better know by it's station abbreviation "HGTV," you edit the hyperlink label to reflect the more accurate name. While in the Edit Hyperlink dialog box, you decide to edit the screen tips associated with the hyperlinks to make them more informative. When finished, you save the file.

What You Do	How You Do It
1. Edit the "Home & Garden Television" hyperlink label to read *HGTV*.	a. **Right-click anywhere on the Home & Garden Television hyperlink** to display the shortcut menu.
	b. **Choose Edit→Hyperlink.**
	c. In the Text To Display box, **replace the existing text with *HGTV*.**
2. Create a custom screen tip for the HGTV hyperlink that reads *Click here to visit Home & Garden Television on the Web.*	a. **Click ScreenTip** ScreenTip... .
	b. In the Set Hyperlink ScreenTip dialog box, **type *Click here to visit Home & Garden Television on the Web.***
	c. **Click OK twice** to accept the screen tip and to edit the hyperlink.

3. Display and observe the HGTV hyperlink's screen tip and then create similar screen tips for the Microsoft HomeAdvisor and Bob Vila's Home Site hyperlinks.

   a. Position your mouse over the HGTV hyperlink. The new screen tip appears.

   b. Display the Edit Hyperlink dialog box for the Microsoft Home Advisor hyperlink.

   c. Display the Set Hyperlink ScreenTip dialog box, and type *Click here to visit Microsoft HomeAdvisor on the Web.*

   d. Click OK twice.

   e. Follow steps b through d to create a screen tip for Bob Vila's Home Site that says *Click here to visit Bob Vila on the Web.*

   f. Save the file.

TOPIC E

Apply a Theme to a Web Page

Once you have created your Web page, you may want to dress it up—depending upon the Web page's purpose. Not an art major? Not to worry. You can add visual interest to your Web pages by applying a collection of formatting attributes to a Web page. In this topic you will apply a built-in unified design element and color scheme to enhance your Web page.

Because you want your Web pages to present a consistent and professional message, you may want to apply color schemes, font choices, and other design elements to them. Word offers a collection of these formatting attributes, called themes, to add visual enhancements to your Web pages all at once. Choosing a theme that is easy to read in a Web browser and one that is appropriate for your business can save you time and provide wonderful results!

Themes

Once you have created your Web page, you may want to add some appropriate formatting to jazz it up.

Definition: *Themes* are a collection of complementary color schemes, font choices, and other design elements that, when applied, automatically provide your Web pages (and documents) with a consistent and professional look.

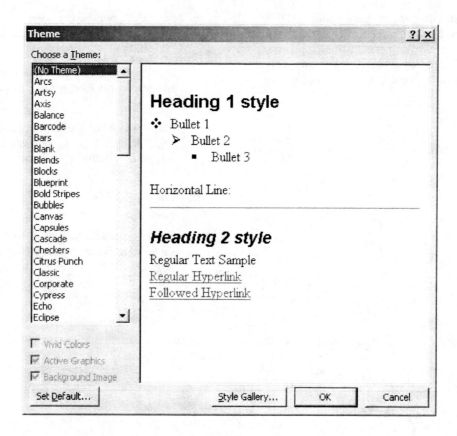

Figure 6-1: *The Themes Dialog box.*

Example: Examples include Blueprint, Rice Paper, and Willow.

Non-Example: A template. If you're familiar with templates, themes may at first sound similar to templates. However themes are different because they affect only how a Web page looks on screen and that's it. They don't contain AutoText, macros, or toolbars that are commonly found in templates.

Apply a Theme to a Web Page

Procedure Reference   When you're selecting a theme, choose one that makes your text easy to read in a Web browser and one that is appropriate for your business. To apply a theme:

1. Choose Format→Theme.

2. From the Choose A Theme list box, select an appropriate theme.

3. Click OK.

     📌 To remove a theme, follow the steps above, except in step 2, select the option No Theme from the Choose A Theme list box.

Activity 6-5

Applying a Theme to a Web Page

Setup: My Simple Web Page.htm is open in Word.

Scenario: After reviewing My Simple Web Page.htm, you decide it could use some jazzing up. Rather than applying individual formatting to the various page elements, you decide to apply one of Word's themes to it. When finished you save and close the file.

What You Do	How You Do It
1. Apply the Blends theme to the Web page.	a. Choose Format→Theme.
	b. From the Choose A Theme list, **observe the Sample box as you select various themes.**
	c. **Select Blends.**
	d. **Click OK.**
2. Display and observe the Web page in the browser.	a. Choose File→Web Page Preview.
	b. If necessary, **maximize the browser window.**
	c. **Return to Word and save and close the file.**

Lesson 6 Follow-up

Because the Internet has become commonplace, you may want to share information using it. Therefore, in this lesson you created and saved a Web page in Word. You added and edited hyperlinks in the Web page and applied a theme in order to enhance it.

1. When creating a Web page in Word, why should you preview it in a browser prior to posting it on the Web?

2. How will you use hyperlinks to enhance your Web pages?

LESSON 7
Managing Document Changes

Data Files:
Comments.doc
Beth.doc
James.doc
Beth.doc
Jonathon.doc
Sarah.doc

Lesson Time:
20–30 minutes

Lesson Objectives:

In this lesson, you will include comments in a document and compare and merge documents.

You will:

*   view, insert, and edit document comments.
*   compare and merge documents.

Introduction

If you've ever had to manage a document with several contributors or editors, you know what a challenge it can be to keep track of who made what change and when. Word offers many tools for tracking these types of changes. In this lesson you will learn about two such collaboration tools—adding electronic comments to documents and comparing and merging documents.

In today's business world it isn't unusual for documents to go through several rounds of revision. The revision process may include just one person, or many. Knowing how to use Word's basic collaboration tools can make your job easier by helping you keep your documents up-to-date and ensuring that they include all the appropriate information.

TOPIC A

Use Comments in Word Documents

While editing or reviewing documents, you may find the need to ask the writer a question or just leave yourself a reminder. Although there are many ways you could get your suggestions to the writer, none is as simple as inserting a comments. Word allows you to add these comments electronically, without altering what the originator wrote. In this topic you will view, insert, and edit comments.

You can use comments to store alternative text, criticisms, ideas for other topics, research notes, and other information useful in developing a document. Adding electronic comments is easy and can save time by avoiding missed phone calls, writing on sticky notes, or catching up with people who are on the go. Suppose that your manager, Jan Burke, is working from home today. She sent you a document for your review via email, and asks that you inform her of any comments that you may have regarding the document. Since you don't want to bother her with a phone call, you add your comments directly to the document and attach it to an email.

Comments

A *comment* is a note or annotation that an author or reviewer adds to a document that is displayed either in a balloon or in the Reviewing Pane. Comments can be used to store alternative text, criticisms, ideas for other topics, research notes, and other information useful in developing a document.

Use Comments in Word Documents

Procedure Reference
To insert a comment:

1. Select the text or object that you want to comment on, or click at the end of the text.

2. Choose Insert→Comment.

3. Type your comment in the comment balloon.

4. Click away from the comment balloon to return to the document text.

✐ If the comment balloons are hidden, you can type the comment in the Reviewing pane.

The Review-ing Toolbar

When you insert a comment, the Reviewing toolbar, shown in Figure 7-1, is automatically displayed. Use screen tips to identify each button.

Figure 7-1: *The Reviewing toolbar.*

Delete Comments

You can delete a comment one of several ways:

- Display the comments shortcut menu, and choose Delete Comment.

- Click on the New Comment button's drop-down arrow and choose Delete Comment.

- In the Reviewing pane, display the comments shortcut menu, and choose Delete Comment.

However, if you delete a comment made by another reviewer and Track Changes is on, the comment will display a strike-through marker.

ACTIVITY 7-1

Using Comments in Word Documents

Setup: Word is running with no files open.

Scenario: Suppose that your manager is working from home today. She has sent you a document, Comments.doc, for your review via email. You open it, view an existing comment, and then add a comment of your own. You then edit your comment in the Reviewing pane and save the file as My Comments.doc.

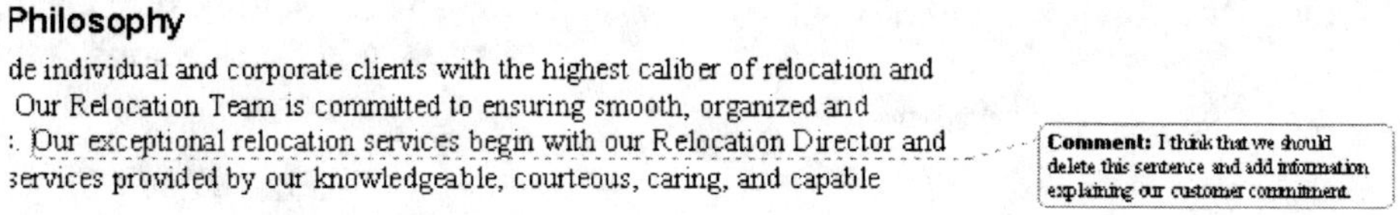

Philosophy

de individual and corporate clients with the highest caliber of relocation and
Our Relocation Team is committed to ensuring smooth, organized and
: Our exceptional relocation services begin with our Relocation Director and
services provided by our knowledgeable, courteous, caring, and capable

> **Comment:** I think that we should delete this sentence and add information explaining our customer commitment.

Figure 7-2: *A document comment.*

What You Do	How You Do It
1. In Comments.doc, observe the existing comment and identify the originator. Add a comment to the word "nationwide" near the end of the "Our Company Affiliations" paragraph that says: *Make sure that all affiliations are included.*	a. **Open and observe** Comments.doc. b. **Display the screen tip for the comment.** The author, date, and time of a comment is listed. **Software Manager, 8/13/2001 4:29 PM:** Commented c. Under "Our Company Affiliations," **select the text "nationwide."** d. **Choose Insert→Comment.** When you insert a comment, Word automatically displays the Reviewing toolbar. Once displayed, you can insert a comment by clicking on the New Comment button 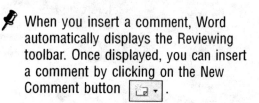 . e. In the Comment balloon, **type** *Make sure that all affiliations are included.* f. **Click away from the comment.**
2. **Display the Reviewing pane and edit your comment to read** *Make sure that all "current" affiliations are included.* **Close the Reviewing pane.**	a. On the Reviewing toolbar, **click on the Reviewing Pane button** 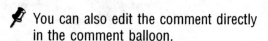 . b. In the Reviewing Pane, **edit your comment to include the word** *current* **before the word "affiliations."** You can also edit the comment directly in the comment balloon. c. **Close the Reviewing pane.** (Click on the Reviewing Pane button.) d. **Save the file as** My Comments.doc. e. **Close the file.**

TOPIC B

Compare and Merge Documents

Keeping track of document changes can get the calmest of people overwhelmed. Having multiple persons reviewing the same document can get your head spinning. Word offers two features for helping with revision management. In this topic you will learn how to compare similar documents, and how to combine documents.

Perhaps you and a co-worker edit separate copies of the same document and then have to create a single document that includes both sets of edits. This task could be a real challenge if you had to cut and paste and keep track of subtle differences between the two documents. However, with Word's compare and merge features it's a much simpler task.

Compare and Merge

If you have two different copies of a document, you can have Word compare or merge the two copies. When these features are used, Word uses change marking to indicate the differences between the documents that you are comparing or the merged text resulting from merging documents.

The *compare documents* feature determines and marks the differences between two documents. Occasionally, you might want to compare an original document to an edited copy just to see what has been changed. If the changes are small, it can be difficult to identify the differences quickly by just looking at the two documents side by side. However, if you use the Compare Documents feature, Word will identify the changes for you by marking the revisions in the open document. The text that differs is displayed in color. Deleted text has a line through it, new text is underlined, and a vertical line at the left margin indicates changed lines in the document.

The *merge documents* feature will combine multiple documents into one document, marking the differences between them. If several reviewers have added comments or edited different copies of a document, you may want to merge all of their comments and tracked changes into one document. This way you can go over all of their marks at once.

Compare and Merge Documents

Comparing Documents

To compare two documents:

1. Open one of the documents you want to compare.

2. Choose Tools→Compare and Merge Documents.

3. In the Compare and Merge Documents dialog box, select the second document for the comparison.

4. Check the Legal Blackline option.

5. If you want Word to mark formatting differences, check the Find Formatting option.

6. Click Compare.

Merging Documents

To merge two documents:

1. Open either of the documents you want to merge, referred to as the first document going forward.

2. Choose Tools→Compare and Merge Documents.

3. In the Compare and Merge Documents dialog box, select the second document you want to merge.

4. In the Compare and Merge Documents dialog box, clear the Legal Blackline check box.

5. If you want Word to mark formatting differences so that later you can choose which formatting to use wherever there's a difference, check the Find Formatting option.

6. In the Compare and Merge Documents dialog box, do one of the following:

   • To overwrite the second document with the resulting merged document, click Merge. The first document will remain as is.

   • To overwrite the first document with the resulting merged document, click the down-arrow on the Merge button and choose Merge Into Current Document. The second document will remain as is.

   • To store the merged document in a new file, click the down-arrow on the Merge button and choose Merge Into New Document. Both the first and second documents will remain as they are.

Reviewing and Incorporating Changes

Now that you can see the changes that were made to the document, you might want to review them and determine if they should be incorporated into the document. Accepting a change makes the change part of your document. Rejecting a change leaves the text as is. To accept or reject changes, use the buttons on the Reviewing toolbar:

1. Place your insertion point at the beginning of the document.

2. If necessary, display the Reviewing toolbar by right-clicking on the Standard toolbar and selecting Reviewing.

3. On the Reviewing toolbar, click on the Next button [⇥] to move to the first change.

4. Depending on whether or not you want to accept or reject the change, click on either the Accept button [✓ ▾] or the Reject button [✗ ▾].

5. Repeat steps 3–4 until all changes are reviewed.

ACTIVITY 7-2

Comparing Documents

Setup: Word is running with no files open.

Scenario: You've been given two documents, Beth.doc and James.doc. Although you've looked at both, you're finding it difficult to identify the differences between the two. So, you decide to use the compare feature. Once you have compared the two documents, you accept all of the document changes and save the file as My Beth.doc. You then close all open files.

What You Do	How You Do It
1. **Compare the two documents Beth.doc and James.doc.**	a. **Open the document** Beth.doc.
	b. **Choose Tools→Compare and Merge Documents.**
	c. **In the Compare and Merge Documents dialog box, select** James.doc.
	d. **Check the Legal Blackline option.**
	e. **Click Compare.**
	f. **Scroll through the** Beth.doc, viewing the markups.
	The text that differs is displayed in color. Deleted text has a line through it, new text is underlined, and a vertical line at the left margin indicates changed lines in the document.

2. **Accept all of the changes made in the document.**

   a. On the Reviewing toolbar, **click on the Accept Change buttons drop-down arrow** 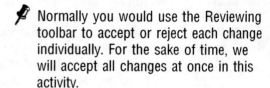 .

   b. **Select Accept All Changes In Document.**

     🖈 Normally you would use the Reviewing toolbar to accept or reject each change individually. For the sake of time, we will accept all changes at once in this activity.

   c. **Save the file as** My Beth.doc.

   d. **Close all files.**

ACTIVITY 7-3

Merging Documents

Setup: Word is running with no files open.

Scenario: Three of Jan Burke's subordinates have edited a letter to a potential client. Jan has asked that you perform the merge, save the merged file, and give it to her for review. The files are: Beth.doc, Jonathon.doc, and Sarah.doc. Once merged, you save the file as My Merged Beth.doc and close all files.

What You Do	How You Do It
1. **Merge the two documents** Beth.doc **and** Jonathon.doc.	a. **Open the file** Beth.doc
	b. In the Compare and Merge Documents dialog box, **select** Jonathon.doc.
	c. **Clear the Legal Blackline option.**
	d. **Click Merge.**

2. **Now merge** Sarah.doc. with the other two files.

a. In the Compare and Merge Documents dialog box, **select** Sarah.doc.

b. **Click on Merge.** The second merged document markings show up in a different color.

c. **Save the file as** My Merged Beth.doc **and close all files without saving the changes.**

Lesson 7 Follow-up

When reviewing documents, you may need to add an electronic comment or compare documents in order to find differences. In this lesson you worked electronic comments, and compared and merged documents.

1. **When might you use comments in Word?**

2. **When might you compare documents?**

3. **When might you merge documents?**

Course Follow-up

Once you have completed this course, you will have the skills necessary to create custom templates and styles, manage tables, insert graphics, and create a newsletter. You will also know how to send form letters using Words' mail merge feature. And, when working with document change management, you will be able to add electronic comments and compare and merge documents.

What's Next?

After completing this course, students may be interested in expanding their knowledge of Microsoft Word by taking elementk's Microsoft Word 2002: Level 3 course.

SOLUTIONS

Lesson 1

Activity 1-1

2. **What Style is applied to the heading "About Us?"**

The Heading1 style has been applied to the About Us heading.

4. **What are some of the available options from the Formatting of Selected Text drop-down menu?**

Select all instances of where a style is used within the document, clear formatting, create a new style, modify a style, promote or demote styles, and display the Reveal Formatting task pane.

Activity 1-3

3. **What has changed in the document?**

The Headings appear underlined, and the Heading 2 style will now apply underlining.

Activity 1-5

1. **In Burke Memo.doc, what would you change before saving the file as a template file?**

Answers will vary but may include deleting the memo address text entries, replacing the from field text, and deleting the memo body text

7. **What type of file appears in the active document window?**

Microsoft Word opens the template as a document file with a temporary name.

8. **Suppose that you now want to enter the information for a new memo. Once entered, how would you save this file?**

Choose File, Save As, type in new file name, and verify that the Save As Type list box is set to "Word Document(.doc).*

Lesson 2

Activity 2-1

2. **How does this table compare with the tabbed driving directions?**

Answers will vary, but may include that the directions are much easier to read now that they are in a table format.

Activity 2-2

3. **Is this the affect that you had intended? Can you think of a solution?**

No, this is not the intended look. A possible solution is to merge the cells in the header row.

Activity 2-3

2. **How is the Excel worksheet data displayed?**

The Excel worksheet data has been converted to a Word table and is displayed in a new Word document with a temporarily assigned name—Sort Rates.xls.

Activity 2-6

2. **What elements are on your screen?**

You now have a Datasheet representing your table data, a bar chart representing the datasheet data, and your table.

Lesson 4

Activity 4-1

3. **What changes occur as a result of Normal view?**

The Styles Area is displayed and section breaks appear as double-lines.

4. **What does the status bar indicate regarding sections?**

The status bar indicates the number of document sections, for example, "Sec 3" indicates the third document section.

6. **Have the margins changed for the other two sections?**

No, the margin change only affected the heading/subheading section settings.

Activity 4-2

3. **Did you get the results you expected?**

   Answers will vary. However, several of the columns break in inconvenient spots.

Activity 4-4

2. **How does the text around the image look?**

   The text may look awkward.

Lesson 5

Activity 5-1

1. **List some examples of main documents that you encounter in your life.**

   Answers will vary, but may include: credit card application form letters, junk email, and catalogs.

Activity 5-2

2. **What appears in the task pane area of your screen?**

   Step 1 of the Mail Merge task pane.

3. **Based on the scenario above, what type of document do we want to work on?**

   Letter.

Activity 5-3

1. **List some examples of data sources that you encounter in your life.**

   Answers will vary, but may include: your Microsoft Outlook Contact list, a paper address book, your local telephone book. a Microsoft Access or Excel database that contains names and addresses.

Activity 5-4

3. What is contained in the Mail Merge Recipients dialog box, shown in Figure 5-4?

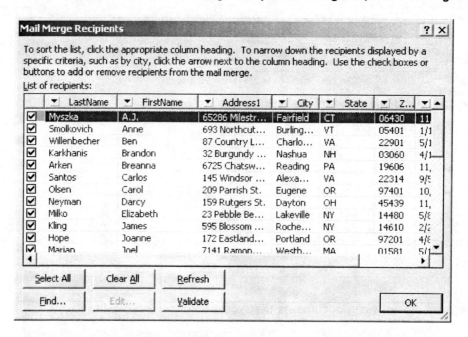

Figure 5-4: *The Mail Merge Recipients dialog box.*

All of the data from the Excel worksheet.

4. What order is the data in? (If necessary, use the scroll bars in the Mail Merge Recipients dialog box to view all of the data.)

The data is in alphabetical order by first name.

Activity 5-5

2. What is contained in the Mail Merge Recipients dialog box shown in Figure 5-5?

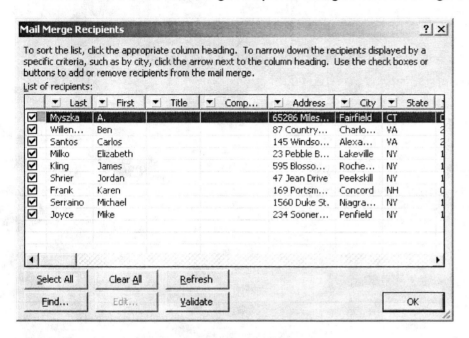

Figure 5-5: *The Mail Merge Recipients dialog box.*

All of the data from the Outlook Contacts folder.

3. What order is the data in? (If necessary, use the scroll bars in the Mail Merge Recipients dialog box to view all of the data.)

The data is in the order in which it was entered.

Activity 5-8

1. What has changed in the document window?

The merge fields now contain data source information for the first record in the data source, Breanna Arken.

Activity 5-9

2. Microsoft Word supports hundreds of label types. What type of labels do you currently use at work?

Answers will vary and may include Avery A4 and A5 sizes or Avery standard.

9. How do your labels compare with Figure 5-12?

Answers will vary.

Lesson 6

Activity 6-2

3. **What is the purpose of the table at the bottom of the Web page?**

This table refers visitors to related information.

Activity 6-3

3. **What indication do you get that the hyperlink has been inserted?**

The text is generally (but not always) underlined and blue. And, if you point directly to it, a screen tip is displayed.

GLOSSARY

balanced columns
Columns that have roughly equal amounts of text in each column.

callout
Text used to call attention to pictures and graphics.

clip art
Professionally designed images that you can add to documents. You can change the size, appearance, and location of clip art after it has been inserted in a document.

Clip Organizer
A gallery of drawings, photographs, sounds, videos, and other media files that you can use in your documents.

column break
A manual break you can insert to determine where one column will end and where the next column will begin.

comment
A note or annotation that an author or reviewer adds to a document that is displayed either in a balloon or in the Reviewing Pane.

compare documents
A Word feature that determines and marks the differences between two documents.

data source
In a Word mail merge, the file that contains the information to be merged into the output document. For example, a Microsoft Excel workbook that contains a list of names or addresses.

drawing canvas
An area upon which you can draw, arrange, and move multiple shapes. It is inserted around some drawings, such as AutoText and organization charts, when you create them.

Drawing objects
Graphics such as curves, lines, AutoShapes, WordArt drawing objects, and diagrams that you draw or insert. These objects are part of your Word document.

Drawing toolbar
Used to create and format many different types of graphic objects. It also contains tools to modify those objects by adding colors, patterns, borders, and other effects.

embedded object
Information that is contained in a source file and inserted into a destination file. Once embedded, the object becomes part of the destination file. Changes you make to the embedded object are reflected only in the destination file.

filter
A set of selection criteria that allows you to include (or exclude) specific data records in a merge.

formula
Mathematical equations that perform calculations in Word tables.

hyperlink
An object, text or a graphic, that links to another Web page. By clicking on the hyperlinked object, you can call that resource up in your browser.

GLOSSARY

line break character

A character you insert by pressing [Shift]+[Enter] to force a new line break manually without creating a new paragraph.

linked object

An object that is created in a source file and inserted into a destination file, while maintaining a connection between the two files. A linked object in the destination file can be updated when the source file is updated.

mail merge

A feature that can be used to personalize form letters and similar documents, as well as to simplify large or repetitive tasks, such as producing catalogs, envelopes, and mailing labels by combining specified data in a generic form.

Mail Merge Wizard

A Word feature that walks you through the necessary steps for performing a mail merge. When accessed, the Mail Merge task pane is displayed.

mailing label

A label that is used in place of an address on a mailed document.

main document

In a Word mail merge, the document that contains the content, text and graphics, that doesn't change from recipient to recipient. For example, the main document would contain the main body of a letter and a letter closing.

merge documents

A Word feature that combines multiple documents into one document, marking the differences between them.

merge fields

In a Word mail merge, a placeholder that instructs Microsoft Word to insert text, graphics, page numbers, and other material into the main document automatically.

Newsletter columns

A layout tool used to control text flow within a document.

Normal style

The Normal style sets the font (Times New Roman), style (regular), size (12 point), color (automatic [black]), and paragraph alignment (left) for every new document opened.

organization chart

Type of diagram that shows hierarchical relationships, such as those between managers, employees, and coworkers.

Organizer

A tool that gives you the ability to manage and share your AutoText entries, styles, toolbars, and macro projects between documents and templates.

orphan

When the first line of a paragraph shows up at the bottom of a page by itself, that line is called an orphan.

pictures

Graphics such as bitmaps, scanned pictures and photographs, and clip art, which are stored in another file.

section

A portion of a document that can have unique page formatting options that are separate from the surrounding document, thereby allowing you to vary page setup features within a document.

section break

A nonprinting double line you insert when you want to create a new section.

style

A set of formatting instructions that can be applied quickly to format text, tables, and lists in your document automatically and consistently. Styles can be applied at either the character or paragraph level.

Styles and Formatting task pane

A task pane used to create, view, and reapply styles.

theme
A collection of complementary color schemes, font choices, and other design elements that, when applied, automatically provide your Web pages (and documents) with a consistent and professional look.

Uniform Resource Locator (URL)
A way to identify the physical location, or address, of a resource that's connected to the Web.

widow
When the last line of a paragraph shows up at the top of a page by itself, that line is called a widow

WordArt
A tool you can use to create unique text effects. Text objects you create with ready-made effects to which you can apply additional formatting options.

NOTES

INDEX

INDEX

callout, 53
clip art, 48, 49
drawing, 54
Drawing objects, 48
Drawing tool, 53
inserting, 48
pictures, 48
WordArt, 57
wrapping text, 79

H
hyperlink
  creating, 123
  editing, 125

L
labels
  creating, 82
  mailing labels, 112

M
mail merge
  data source, 94, 99
  identifying main document, 88
  Mail Merge Wizard, 90
  merge fields, 103
mailing labels
  creating, 112
merge fields
  inserting, 103

N
newletter
  section break, 68
newsletter
  controlling text flow, 77
  formatting columns, 74
  formatting text, 74
  labels, 82
  newsletter, 82
  envelopes
  newsletter columns, 74
  section, 68
  sectioning, 68
  wrapping text, 79

O
Organization Chart
  editing, 61

S
section
  creating, 70
sections
  inserting, 68
styles
  applying, 2
  creating, 13
  deleting, 13
  formatting, 2
  modifying, 10
  normal style, 2
  Styles and Formatting Task Pane, 3
  types, 2
  user-defined, 13

T
table
  sorting data, 31
tables
  converting tabbed text, 24
  embedding, 42
  Embedding Object, 42
  Excel, 29
  formula, 33
  Header Row, 27
  linking data, 42
  Linking Object, 42
  managing, 24
  merging cells, 27
  opening in Word, 29
  performing, 33, 34
templates
  applying styles, 2
  creating, 17
    from existing document
  modifying styles, 10
  Organizer, 17
  user-defined styles, 13
themes
  applying, 127

NOTES